FASHION WRITING
AND CRITICISM

FASHION WRITING AND CRITICISM

History, Theory, Practice

PETER McNEIL and SANDA MILLER

B L O O M S B U R Y

LONDON • NEW DELHI • NEW YORK • SYDNEY

Bloomsbury Academic

An imprint of Bloomsbury Publishing Plc

50 Bedford Square
London
WC1B 3DP
UK

1385 Broadway
New York
NY 10018
USA

www.bloomsbury.com

Bloomsbury is a registered trade mark of Bloomsbury Publishing Plc

First published 2014

© Peter McNeil and Sanda Miller, 2014

Peter McNeil and Sanda Miller have asserted their right under the Copyright, Designs and
Patents Act, 1988, to be identified as Authors of this work.

British Library Cataloguing-in-Publication Data
A catalogue record for this book is available from the British Library.

ISBN: HB: 978-0-8578-5446-9
PB: 978-0-8578-5447-6
ePDF: 978-0-8578-5472-8
ePub: 978-0-8578-5471-1

Library of Congress Cataloging-in-Publication Data
Fashion writing and criticism : history, theory, practice / Peter McNeil, Sanda Miller
pages cm
Includes bibliographical references and index.
ISBN 987-0-85785-447-6 (paperback) — ISBN 978-0-85785-446-9 (hardback —
ISBN 978-0-85785-471-1 (epub) 1. Fashion writing. I. Miller, Sanda. II. Title.
TT503.5.M36 2014
808.06'674692—dc23
2014010306

Typeset by RefineCatch Limited, Bungay, Suffolk
Printed and bound in India

CONTENTS

LIST OF IMAGES

ACKNOWLEDGEMENTS

This book began life, as many seem to do, around a breakfast table. It was in Putney, London, on a May morning several years ago. Valerie Steele had first brought us together, at one of her innovative symposia held at the Fashion Institute of Technology in New York. Peter talked about women lusting after shoes, and Sanda on the dodgy ontology of fashion criticism. A flute of champagne that evening, and a friendship developed.

We wish to thank our families and friends for their support during the writing of this work. Particular thanks go to our many London based friends, Ian Henderson, Kwesi Edman, and our mutual Swiss friend Martin Kamer. To the gentlemen at Diktats Bookstore, Paris, Monsieur Antoine and Monsieur Nicolas, we are also indebted. We thank the current and former staff at *Acne Paper*, and Erika Lunding, Stockholm. We owe a debt to museum curators and assistants, including Valerie Steele, Patricia Mears and Melissa Marra (Fashion Institute of Technology, New York); Pamela Parmal (Museum of Fine Arts, Boston); and Roger Leong and Jennie Moloney (National Gallery of Victoria). The staff of the Lewis Walpole Library, Yale University, particularly Susan Odell Walker, have been most helpful. Thanks go to Thi Nguyen for sharing his work. Peter also thanks the intellectual support of the network Fashioning the Early Modern (Humanities in the European Research Area), which ran from 2010 to 2013, and the post-doctoral fellow Dr Patrik Steorn (now Director of Thielska Museet). He is grateful to Giorgio Riello and Richard Read for their encouragement. Sanda also thanks her friend and supporter, Professor Laura Bovone (Universita Cattolica, Milan). Joanna Kalkstein lent Peter the use of the inspirational stone walls of 'Coomassie' in the Blue Mountains for the final stage of editing.

Finally we thank our employers, the University of Technology Sydney (and in particular Professor Desley Luscombe), Stockholm University, as well as Southampton Solent University, specifically professors Jane Longmore, Rod Piling and Maurice Owen; and Istituto Marangoni (London), specifically Monica Cattorini (director of the London campus), Adrien Parry Roberts (director of academic education) and Sanda's special colleague and friend Filippo Piccardi.

Peter dedicates this book to Simon Lee, who reads fashion blogs daily, and Sanda to Noa, Giulia and Neil for being family.

Parts of the research contained in this book have been supported by grants from the Centre for Contemporary Design Practices, University of Technology, Sydney; 'Fashioning the Early Modern: Creativity and Innovation in Europe c.1500–1800', Humanities in the European Research Area (HERA): 'Humanities as a Source of Creativity and Innovation', leader Professor Evelyn Welch; Peter McNeil's project therein: 'Print Culture and Fashion Products'; and the funding agency Vetenskaprådet (SE) (Sweden). The work was also supported by a Visiting Fellowship for Peter at the Lewis Walpole Library, Yale University.

PART ONE

WHAT IS CRITICISM?

1
INTRODUCTION

We are surrounded by criticism, including the critique of fashion, but why is the quality of writing about fashion so uneven? 'Criticism' emerged through literature and the fine arts. It has since expanded to such an extent that we are expected today to be critical of our restaurant meals, our bathroom fittings and our sartorial fashions, although in the strict sense of the word, the remit of criticism is generally accepted to be the art world.

What does the critic do? How do we acquire the skill set to be active critics? In other words, who are the critics, how do we 'become' critics, and what qualities are required to act as a critic? Above all, how do we recognize quality fashion criticism and why is it so narrowly focused and subjective at the moment? The answer is staring us in the face: we are accustomed to reading fashion journalism that amounts to no more than excited description and personal opinion, much of it being media-led accolades or 'badmouthing'. This would not be tolerated within the fine arts, literature, the theatre or film. How might we develop a proper critical vocabulary for fashion writing, which transcends this level and will enable us to understand, assess and above all make value judgements about something as changeable as fashion?

These are the key questions that are asked here. This is the first book to connect shifts in critical writing and approaches to fashion over a long span of time, from the seventeenth century to the present day. Beginning with the power of Aristotle's *Poetics*, it explains that the plot – which is the most important of the six constituent parts of the 'tragedy' – is, after all, story telling, but story telling to be compelling must have drama and embody insights. Why did evaluative thinking emerge at all? What does criticism mean? How did criticism expand beyond the fine arts to the camera and other new media? How did the great critics reflect on the social, artistic and aesthetic changes that revolutionized fashion since the first texts about sartorial dress were published in the first fashion magazines of the late-seventeenth and eighteenth centuries? The role of taste in eighteenth-century philosophical aesthetics will be directly related to assessments of fashion in that period. How did a judicial (evaluative) vocabulary for fashion journalism emerge in the nineteenth century and where did it lead?

This introduction considers the emergence during the eighteenth century of the 'modern system of the arts': the twin disciplines of aesthetics and art history, and art criticism as a convenient starting point for this inquiry. These terms are explained through the lens derived from the Renaissance scholar P.O. Kristeller regarding the hierarchy of the arts. In it he undertakes to demonstrate that the 'system of the five major arts, which underlies all modern aesthetics and is so familiar to us all, is of comparatively recent origin and did not assume definite shape before the eighteenth century' (Kristeller, 1961, p. 165). Kristeller starts with the ancients, who regarded poetry as the most highly respected form of art, followed by music and then the three visual arts: painting, sculpture and architecture (Kristeller, 1961). After an elegant journey throughout history, Kristeller located the genesis of the grouping together of the visual arts with poetry and music during the eighteenth century. Although he accepts that 'it is not easy to indicate the causes for the genesis of the system in the eighteenth century', he nevertheless identifies a few key factors:

> the rise of painting and of music since the Renaissance, not so much in their actual achievements as in their prestige and appeal, the rise of literary and art criticism, and above all the rise of an amateur public to which art collections and exhibitions, concerts as well as opera and theatre performances were addressed, must be considered as important factors (Kristeller, 1961, p. 225).

The proper domain of the critic is tripartite: it involves description, interpretation and evaluation. These basic aspects of criticism do not simply concern judgement as many think; they include the historical (Roger Fry on the painter Paul Cézanne), the re-creative (Walter Pater on the Renaissance polymath Leonardo da Vinci) and the judicial, supplying a set of standards or canons (F.R. Leavis, T.S. Eliot and Harold Bloom on literature). The latter includes topics such as 'truth', 'morality' or 'artistic significance', but such standards must be appropriate for the object of study. The notion of re-creative criticism as a 'work of art' in its own right is central here. Examples will be provided in this book from the classic writers who approach criticism in these different ways. The purpose here is to explain that criticism is not simply 'opinion'.

The book will explain criticism generally and in a straightforward manner from its beginning and development in antiquity to the present day. It will explore the role of value judgements in assessing the job of the fashion critic, and relate the philosophical issue of moving from the 'subjective' to the 'objective', and how this might be achieved in fashion writing today. It will challenge and more importantly *explain* the dominance of subjective approaches ('opinion') in contemporary fashion journalism. What can be done in a concrete fashion to move beyond the level of the public relations department and the press release, important agents as they are in the creation of the fashion system? What type of critical writing might enable real change in what many view as an unsustainable industry? Will the critic disappear under the weight of blogs and tweets or will it blossom within new media?

The work is divided into two parts. The first, 'What is Criticism?', charts the emergence of criticism and its operations from the classical world to the twenty-first century. How did criticism emerge? Why did evaluative thinking develop and what is the rational basis for such a seemingly subjective activity? What role did criticism play in Ancient Athenian society? Criticism re-emerged, but shifted from the Aristotelian literary to visual arts criticism with the founding of the Académie royale de peinture et de sculpture by Louis XIV in 1648 and the subsequent establishment of the Enlightenment *salons* as the first public space for critical debate. During this period, 'philosophical aesthetics' emerged as an independent branch of philosophy.

Centre stage to our project is the concept of 'taste' (the French word is *goût*). Taste, which was one of the cornerstones of philosophical aesthetics, itself a product of the Enlightenment, has very much fallen from view in our times of 'fast fashion'. To ask a person in the street 'what is your taste?' is likely to result in puzzlement, as it does not concern what brands you intend to buy. Yet in the past, taste was directly related to assessments of fashion; indeed the very notion gave fashion a new gravitas during the Enlightenment. Fashion and taste were a significant part of this fervent debate, to the extent that we find them making a mark in the famous *Encyclopédie* (1751–72) penned by Denis Diderot and Jean le Rond d'Alembert. The *philosophe* Diderot, prompted by his friend Melchior von Grimm, whose job it was to report to Frederick II, King of Prussia, concerning French artistic and cultural life, created the form of a journal, *Corréspondence littéraire, philosophique et critique*, which circulated in manuscript form. In it von Grimm started to report on the biennial *salons* that exhibited painting and sculpture, but eventually persuaded his friend Diderot to take over his reviews of the *salons* between 1759 and 1771, with two final contributions in 1775 and 1781, which were eventually published in book form as *Salons*. Imagination, taste and aesthetic pleasure were debated in the coffee houses of London and the fashionable drawing-rooms of Paris, Berlin and Stockholm. The term 'taste' was appropriated in the titles and texts of almost all eighteenth-century fashion magazines, the evidence for an argument about which is made here forcefully for the first time.

During the nineteenth century, the poet Charles Baudelaire, whose notorious volume of poems *Les fleurs du mal* (1857) shocked bourgeois Paris, took Diderot's pioneering *reportage* of the *salons* a stage further, becoming the first 'professional' art critic. In his seminal essay 'The Painter of Modern Life' (1863), Baudelaire appropriated his own term 'charm', frequently used in his poetry, and put it to a new use by predicating it on fashion: 'all fashions are charming'. This was the first time an evaluative concept was applied to fashion and it marked the beginning of a 'critical vocabulary' of fashion. We argue that this also marked the burgeoning of an 'expanded field' of fashion that was not simply about getting and spending, but concerned the 'poetics' of dress. If fashion might have a poetic dimension, then it can be thought of and written about using different apparatus than the public relations department might provide.

With the concurrent invention of the arts of the camera in the nineteenth century, first photography and later the cinema, we see the emergence of a new debate as to whether such forms can be considered an art at all. As John P. Thompson notes, 'The eighteenth- and nineteenth-century disputes over the artistic value of engravings and photography are indicative of a more fundamental conflict to control the process of economic valorization at a time when the emergence of new technical media were making possible the mass reproduction of symbolic forms' (Thompson, 1990, p. 166). New value judgements thus had to be created in order to understand and evaluate the new media and formats of cultural production, which included fashion, although this was not much remarked at the time of sartorial fashion. This era marked the beginning of the expansion of criticism into things other than the strictly defined 'fine arts'. This in turn legitimized the application of a critical vocabulary of fashion writing, validating fashion as a part of European culture. Such value judgements were also made in new ways, for very different fields – architecture, for example. 'Any opinion expressed about a building or group of buildings can, in its widest sense, be called a rational judgement. In this sense, Ruskin's rapturous assessment of the merits of St. Mark's, Venice, is just as much a reasoned judgement as a surveyor's report on the condition of a mediaeval barn' (Collins, 1971, p. 36) wrote Peter Collins in the early 1970s.

This first part of the book therefore explains how a judicial (evaluative) vocabulary for fashion journalism emerged in the nineteenth century, becoming the bedrock of twentieth-century fashion writing. It also helps to partly explain why fashion retains such a vexed position in contemporary cultural debates. We also offer it as an alternative to the generally stale art or fashion debate that has become turgid and opportunistic in recent years.

This book repudiates the idea that we can simply go to the world wide web in order to write about fashion today. In order to be a critic of fashion, one must first be informed about fashion, in all its complexity: aesthetic, social, cultural, economic and historical. One is rarely sufficient, yet the process of fashion research (now sometimes called 'fashion studies') has tended to be taught using one dominant lens. Such approaches will continue to constrain and restrain academic and wider public understandings of fashion unless wider integration is continually attempted.

The second part of the book, 'Reporting Fashion', takes a case-study approach to fashion writing. This section begins by providing an account of how the critical vocabulary of fashion emerges with terms such as 'brilliant', 'charming', 'gracious', 'elegant', 'glamorous', 'luxurious' and 'de bon ton' in the international fashion magazines of the 1910s and 1920s. What did such terms really mean and why were they omnipresent?

The fact that this book starts from an historical perspective will enable it to transcend the dominant practice of analysing contemporary fashion magazines by focusing on textual and discourse analyses (Conekin and de la Haye, 2006; Lynge-Jorlen, 2012). It further builds on the model of close reading of historical fashion magazines for their imbrication of gender and consumption (Breward, 1994). We propose an alternative approach that integrates history and theory in studying the practice of fashion writing. It will not simply focus on the written word, but also consider 'form'. For example, from the luxurious hand-finished pages of the *Gazette du Bon Ton* (Paris 1912–25) to the production values of *Acne Paper* (contemporary Stockholm), attempts have been made to marry the physical and material aspect of a journal by insisting on the intellectual content in fashion writing and a relationship to layout.

The work thus provides an innovative account of the link between fashion writing, aesthetics, 'taste' and the position of the critic to start with, and subsequently the newly emerging fashion critic within it – not just in the past, but for today's rapidly changing fashion-scape. How might we create today the 'qualified observer' for fashion that David Hume argued for in the arts centuries ago in *Of the Standard of Taste* (1757)? This book will argue that the development of taste was not a matter of mere literary, rhetorical or editorial style, or indeed caprice, but a direct result of the ideological revolution brought about by the Enlightenment. Fashion writing changed forever. This story will be recounted and explained for the first time, linked firmly to the present.

2
ARISTOTLE AND THE ORIGINS OF CRITICISM

All thought is either practical or productive or theoretical.

Aristotle

Aristotle's fourth-century BC *Poetics* is the starting point for criticism and its contemporary application. Aristotle defined tragedy as being divided into the six elements of plot, character, diction, thought, spectacle and song. He provided an explanation of the 'proper pleasure' of tragedy as catharsis (purgation) resulting from pity and fear. For a tragedy to function well he then suggested the three famous unities: action, time and place. Are they of further use to us? The answer is vehemently yes. It would be difficult to read a good film or theatre review in the press today that did not reveal the legacy of Aristotle. Moreover, this venerable work informs the job of the scriptwriter; plot (narrative), dialogue and character all come from Aristotle. If such concepts are the basis of criticism, how can they be applied to fashion? If we accept that fashion may be a form of art, and therefore a newcomer to the pantheon of the sister arts, then a critical vocabulary is necessary to evaluate its aesthetic (artistic) worth. This section explains to the student of fashion how to structure and evaluate critical prose.

The poetics today

A book with the improbable title *Aristotle in Hollywood*, written by Finnish television executive Ari Hiltunen, was first published in the UK in 2002. The very idea of conjoining a Greek philosopher with the American film industry seemed bizarre to say the least, as Chris Vogler, who wrote its preface commented: "'Aristotle in Hollywood?" At first it sounds like the pitch line for a bad time-travel movie. So this Greek guy Aristotle gets conked on the head with an amphora and wakes up in Hollywood where his philosophies are turned into block busters saving a major studio' (Vogler in Hiltunen, 2002, Preface).

While Aristotle never made it to Hollywood as a time traveller to save the film industry from financial trouble, his ideas certainly did, and herein lies the true miracle implied in Vogler's amusing narrative: how can we really explain that Aristotle's little book *Poetics*, written in Athens about 340 BC, continues to hold sway on our modern sensibilities when it comes to not only the theatre, but also movie scriptwriting, best-selling fiction, TV series and even cyberspace?

The answer may appear simple enough; Aristotle understood not only the universal appeal of drama, but more importantly he was the first to offer a psychological explanation of how it worked on our psyche. From this explanation he extracted a set of critical criteria for how to write drama that best fulfilled this specific function. But nothing could be further from the truth, given not only the complex history of *The Poetics*, but also the difficult and obscure terminology that Aristotle employed.

Aristotle's written legacy

In the aftermath of the death of Alexander the Great in 323 BC and the division of his empire, about two-thirds of Aristotle's writings disappeared or were destroyed, and those that were saved were taken to Asia Minor for safe keeping and thence to Rome, where a Greek, Andronicus of Rhodes, prepared a revised edition of the surviving material. First published in 70 BC, it constitutes to date the authoritative corpus of Aristotle's writing.

Aristotle was a prodigious polymath as testified by the variety of subjects he wrote about, and almost certainly taught his students at the Athenian *lyceum*. They included logic, physics, metaphysics, politics, rhetoric, ethics, psychology, and among them a short treatise dedicated to literature: *Poetics*, written around 335 BC. From this treatise, only the first half, dedicated to tragedy and epic poetry, survived; the second part, which contained an analysis of comedy, is lost. It may well be that when Aristotle embarked on writing the *Poetics* he intended it partially as a retaliation against his teacher Plato's rant against the arts (Pappas in Gaut and Lopes, 2001, p. 15) found in one of his most famous dialogues: *The Republic*.

In a seminal essay entitled 'The Fire and the Sun' (why Plato banished the artists)' the distinguished classical philosopher Iris Murdoch argued that for Plato, the arts, which in the Greek context were regarded as mere *technai* (crafts), constituted the lowest and most irrational kind of awareness. This was explained in terms of the 'cave myth', pointing to the condition of the prisoners who face the back wall and instead of seeing the 'real' world, see only shadows cast by the fire (Murdoch, 1977, p. 5).

Plato versus Aristotle on knowledge, the arts and beauty

Plato developed his theories on art and beauty in Books III and X of *The Republic* and reached the uncomfortable conclusion that:

> Artists are interested in what is base and complex, not what is simple and good. They induce the better part of the soul to 'relax its guard'. Thus images of wickedness and excess may lead even good people to indulge secretly through art feelings which they would be ashamed to entertain in real life. We enjoy cruel jokes and bad taste in the theatre, then behave boorishly at home. Art both expresses and gratifies the lowest part of the soul, and feeds and enlivens base emotions which ought to be left to wither (Murdoch, 1977, p. 6).

The question of what motivated Plato's poisonous remarks is simply to do with *episteme* (knowledge); it all amounts to the high regard in which he holds knowledge; given that all the arts (*technai*) are imitations of things in the 'real' world, their knowledge content is negligible, which for Plato was tantamount to immorality, as espoused in Book X of *The Republic.*

Central to this argument is the concept of *mimesis* (imitation), which instead of being provided with a logical definition of the necessary and sufficient conditions for its classification as *mimesis* is explained in typical Socratic style by using an example: Socrates provides a famous and frequently quoted example of the three kinds of beds. The first is 'in nature a bed', the second is 'the work of the carpenter', and the third bed is 'the one that the painter makes' (Plato in Cooper, 1997, p. 1201). Thus a hierarchy is created, starting with the ideal form of the bed, then the bed made by the carpenter, and finally the bed painted by the painter. Socrates accepts that by making a bed that imitates the ideal form of the bed, the carpenter is a maker of a bed, but then the painter is an imitator of what the carpenter makes, and to make matters worse, he imitates only the appearance of the carpenter's physical object, being even further removed from the truth embodied in the essence of the bed. Thus when the painter paints a bed, representing it from a particular angle, such an imitation 'is very far removed from the truth for it touches only a small part of each thing and a part that is itself only an image' (Plato in Cooper, 1997, p. 1202). The painter's bed amounts to no more than: 'an image, which when compared with a real bed and with the Form of Bed, is at two moves from reality, and that to make such an image requires no genuine knowledge; no knowledge of the real things of which one makes an image' (Janaway in Benson, 2009, p. 393).

Aristotle differed significantly from Plato regarding the all-important issue of knowledge (*episteme*) in the two literary categories he analysed in the *Poetics,* drama and epic poetry. Aristotle believed that poetry deals with universals, unlike history, which he regarded as a mere chronicle of facts and dates, and during the heroic times of Herodotus (484–425 BC), regarded as the first historian, this was indeed the case. In that sense the poet must be able to show how actions follow from their proper causes, which presupposes a thorough knowledge of psychological laws (the ability to predict that a person would necessarily or at least probably act in a specific way and not another). Thus Aristotle made the important point that even if the poet does not have knowledge of shipbuilding or military strategy he cannot fake psychological knowledge, namely an understanding of human nature, and only then can the tragedy fulfil its function of being a successful imitation of a human action (Beardsley, 1966, p. 63).

What is tragedy?

Why do people go to see tragedies, which instead of offering pleasurable relief from the tedium of everyday life are full of 'sound and fury'? Consider King Lear's grief when he learns about the death of his daughter Cordelia murdered in prison and his realization of the heinous betrayal of his two other daughters, Goneril and Reagan:

> Howl, Howl, Howl! O, you are men of stones
> Had I your ears and eyes, I'd use them so
> That heaven's vault should crack! She's gone for ever (Shakespeare, 1980, p. 952).

The answer is that the unleashing of such powerful emotions seen from a distance in space and time – they happen on stage and many hundreds of years ago – instead of filling us with dread, fills us with pleasure, but a very special pleasure specific only to tragedy, which is its 'proper' pleasure (*oikeia hedone*), to do with the realization that although such things could happen to us, what we witness is not happening to us in reality. Aristotle then quite naturally wanted to ask a simple question: why are tragedies written at all: what is its final cause (*telos*) or, to put it simply, what is the use of tragedy?

In explaining how anything comes to exist, for example how poetry is created or sculpture is made, Aristotle proposed four causes or explanations – he answered the question 'why?' by postulating four causes or explanations in the creation of an object, which he calls 'material', 'formal', 'efficient' and 'final' (*telos*), which is the most important, because it answers the question: what is the object for?:

> 'Cause' means: (1) that from which, as immanent material, a thing comes into being, e.g. the bronze is the cause of the statue and the silver of the saucer.

(2) The form or pattern, i.e. the definition of the essence, and the classes which include this (e.g. the ratio 2:1 and number in general are causes of the octave), and the parts included in the definition. (3) That form which the change or the resting from change first begins; e.g. the adviser is a cause of the action, and the father a cause of the child, and in general the maker a cause of the thing made and the change-producing of the changing. (4) The end, i.e. that for the sake of which a thing is; e.g. health is the cause of walking. For 'Why does one walk?' we say; 'that one may be healthy'; and in speaking thus we think we have given the cause means the final end, that is, that for the sake of which some thing else is. For instance, health is an end in walking. For why does one walk? 'To be healthy' we say and in so saying think we have named the cause. We think the same of every means employed by some agent to bring about an end (Aristotle in McKeon, *Metaphysics,* 2001: Book V, Chapter 1, 1013a, 20–35, p. 752).

In the instance of writing a tragedy, the final cause (*telos*) for writing is to give pleasure (*agathon*), but it has to be its 'proper' pleasure. And the all important notion of the 'proper pleasure' (*oikeia hedone*) constitutes the starting point for the development of criticism of which we find the most developed account in the *Nichomachean Ethics*. Pleasures are bound with the activities they complete:

For an activity is intensified by its proper pleasure since each class of things is better judged and brought to precision by those who engage in the activity with pleasure e.g. it is those who enjoy geometrical thinking that become geometers and grasp the various propositions better, and, similarly those who are fond of music or of building, and so on, make progress in their proper function by enjoying it; so the pleasures intensify the activities and what intensifies a thing is proper to it, but things different in kind have properties different in kind (Aristotle in McKeon, *Nocomachean Ethics*. 2001, Book X, Chapter 5, 1175, 25–35, p. 1100).

Aristotle then assessed the means by which tragedy produces this proper pleasure and the answer to this question constitutes the starting point for critical evaluation, the key point of the book you are now reading.

Tragedy produces its 'proper pleasure' through imitation (*mimesis*) of an action. Human beings are rational animals and take pleasure in imitation as a special case of learning, which provides also an answer to Plato, who regarded the arts he defined as imitations of imitation, to have the lowest knowledge content possible:

Again, since learning and wondering are pleasant, it follows that such things as acts of imitation must be pleasant – for instance painting, sculpture, poetry – and every product of skilful imitation; this latter, even if the object imitated is not itself pleasant; for it is not the object itself which here gives delight; the spectator draws inferences ('That is a so-and-so') and thus learns something fresh. Dramatic turns of fortunate and hairbreadth escapes from perils are pleasant, because we feel all such things are wonderful (Aristotle in McKeon, 2001: *Rhetoric*, Book I, Chapter 11, 1371b, 1–10, p. 1365).

Furthermore, all imitative arts differ from one another in three respects: the medium, the objects, and the manner or mode of imitation. First, the medium: 'there are persons' Aristotle stated, who imitate and represent various objects through the medium of colour and form, by whom Aristotle meant painters; second, with regard to epic poetry and tragedy, comedy and dithyrambic poetry, and the music of the flute and the lyre, the imitation is produced by 'rhythm, language, or "harmony" either singly or combined' (Butcher, 1951, I 2–4, p. 7) and this belongs to the art of poetry, which 'is distinguished from painting in terms of its medium (words, melody, rhythm) and from versified history or philosophy (the poem of Empedocles) by virtue of the object it imitates' (Beardsley, 1966, p. 55). 'The idea of approaching the problem of critical evaluation by looking for a particular kind of enjoyment that it is the function of a particular art or genre of art, to give, is a very important one. And this seems capable of empirical investigation' (Beardsley, 1966, p. 57).

Aristotle was able to provide a definition of tragedy by considering the psychological impact it makes on the reader or the audience and once this is established he then suggested how the playwright might write a tragedy that would best fulfil its function, that of producing the 'proper pleasure' it is meant to embody.

Tragedy, then, is an imitation of an action that is serious, complete and of a certain magnitude in language, embellished with each kind of artistic ornament, the several kinds being found in separate parts of the play; in the form of action, not of narrative; and through pity and fear effecting the proper purgation of these emotions (Butcher, 1951, VI, 2–3, p. 23).

The two separate issues to be dealt with regarding this seminal definition are the structure of the tragedy and its final cause (*telos*) – effecting the proper purgation (*catharsis*) of the emotions of pity (*eleos*) and fear (*phobos*), which Aristotle defined in *Rhetoric* as species of pain.

Several interpretations of this statement are possible, but the closest Aristotle came to explaining this paradox himself was a comment he made in the *Poetics*, whereby the instinct of imitation is part of human nature and through it we learn our earliest lessons:

And no less universal is the pleasure felt in things imitated. We have evidence of this in the facts of experience. Objects which in themselves we view with pain, we delight to contemplate when reproduced with minute fidelity; such as the forms of the most ignoble animals and of dead bodies. The cause of this again is, that to learn gives the liveliest pleasure, not only to philosophers, but to men in general, whose capacity, however, of learning is more limited (Butcher, 1951, III, 3–5, p. 15).

This is a wonderful statement, not only as a refutation of Plato's disparaging comments about the arts as undesirable in his ideal Republic, but also as confirmation to how much Aristotle valued learning and knowledge not only in themselves but also as a source of wonderful pleasure. And so, whether we view dead animals or witness the unbearable suffering of Oedipus, the pleasure we get should not be regarded either as perverse or immoral, because as imitations they are removed from reality and as spectators, so are we; through *pity* and *fear* to effect the proper purgation: the famous *catharsis* regarded as the most difficult of Aristotle's terms, which he only referred to once in the *Poetics* but has been much repeated over the centuries. The canonical interpretation is generally considered to be the one proposed by H.S. Butcher: 'through pity and fear effecting the proper purgation of these emotions, the implication being that *catharsis* has a therapeutic effect on the audience's mental health, giving a pleasurable sense of relief – "in calm of mind, all passion spent" – as Milton echoes this view in *Samson Agonistes*' (Beardsley, 1966, p. 64). We can now move to the structure of the tragedy from which we can infer the critical criteria of how to write a tragedy whose proper pleasure is to relieve the audience of pity and fear through *catharsis*: a good cry?

The structure of a Greek tragedy

Once the function of tragedy (*catharsis*) has been established, Aristotle derived his critical criteria from the way a tragedy should be put together in order to fulfil its function. His next step was to provide a definition of tragedy: tragedy is an 'imitation of an action', but he refined this basic definition specifically into what kind of action. Tragedy, then, is: 'an imitation of an action that is serious, complete, and of a certain magnitude; in language embellished with each kind of artistic ornament, the several kinds being found in separate parts of the play in the form of action, not of narrative' (Butcher, 1951, V.4 2–3, p. 23).

Specifically, Aristotle argued, a tragedy has six parts that he enlisted according to their hierarchical importance: *plot, character, diction, thought, song* and *spectacle*; plot as the imitator of the action being the most important, while spectacle is regarded as the bottom of the ladder as the least artistic. Aristotle devoted special attention to the plot (*mythos*) or the narrative, specifying how it should be written and thus introducing for the first time critical (evaluative) criteria as guidelines to producing an excellent plot.

Tragedy, also as a unified whole, must have a beginning, a middle and an end (now do you understand the structure of your high school essay?) and while these words appear trivial to the point of reminding us of the reasoning we encounter in Lewis Carroll's *Alice in Wonderland*, this is not the case, because he was specific about how they link with each other:

> a beginning is that which does not itself follow anything by causal necessity, but after which something naturally is or comes to be. And end, on the contrary, is that which itself naturally follows some other thing, either by necessity, or as a rule, but has nothing following it. A middle is that which follows something as some other thing follows it (Butcher, 1951, VI.19 2–4, p. 31).

This is important, because at this point Aristotle introduced the first critical criterion referring to the length of an ideal plot, comparing the well-constructed plot to a beautiful object, such as a living organism, 'or any whole composed of parts', which necessitates not only an orderly structure but a certain magnitude, not too small, because 'a very small animal organism cannot be beautiful; for this view of it is confused', not too large, 'for the eye cannot take it all in at once, the unity and sense of the whole is lost for the spectator'. The magnitude necessary in the case of a living organism and in the plot is that it might be 'easily embraced in one view; so in the plot, a certain length is necessary, and a length which can be easily embraced by the memory' (Butcher, 1951, VI 19 to VII 4–7, pp. 33–4).

Aristotle provided in the *Metaphysics* a definition of beauty as consisting 'in size and arrangement', its chief forms being 'order and symmetry and definiteness'. The Greek definition of beauty travelled through history and took centre stage during the Renaissance in Florence, echoed by the humanist and philosopher Leon Battista Alberti (1404–72) in his book on architecture *De Re Aedificatoria*, which was in turn modelled on Vitruvius' treatise *The Ten Books of Architecture*. In it he argued that beauty in a building consists of three qualities: *numeros* (number), *finitio* (proportion) and *collocatio* (location, disposition, or arrangement), which converge together to produce *concinnitas* (a well-adjusted whole), providing also his famous definition of beauty as consisting in proportion, order, symmetry, which create a self-contained entity that cannot be tampered with but for the worse. Thus beauty consists of 'the harmony of all the members, so that nothing can be taken away or added or changed, except for the worse' (quoted in Watkin, 1986, p. 182).

Aristotle recycled the definition used in *Metaphysics* and applied to tragedy in the *Poetics* but instead of using it as a quality in tragedy that contributes to its artistic value, for example a beautiful tragedy, he used it as 'an aesthetic value predicate', a tragedy worthy of praise, for example 'this is good stuff', and one such would be a tragedy that is orderly in structure and of the right magnitude (Beardsley, 1966, p. 61). The proper magnitude of a tragedy 'is comprised within such limits, that the sequence of events, according to the law of probability or necessity, will admit of a change from bad fortune to good, or from good fortune to bad' (Butcher, 1951, VII 5, 7, p. 33).

Aristotle introduced the first of the 'famous' three unities ('unity of action', 'unity of time', 'unity of place') at this point, arguing that the unity of a plot does not consist 'in the unity of the hero', but as an imitation of an action it 'must imitate one action and that of a whole, the structural union of the parts being such that, if any one of them is displaced or removed, the whole will be disjointed and disturbed' (Butcher, 1951, VIII 3, 4, p. 35). Aristotle divided the plots into simple and complex, the former being the imitation of an action 'which is one and continuous in the sense above defined' and when the change of fortune takes place without reversal and recognition. Reversal (*peripeteia*) and recognition (*agnagorisis*) are two key concepts introduced in the definition of the complex action where change is accompanied by reversal and recognition' (Butcher, 1951, X, 3, 2–3, p. 39).

Aristotle was fond of Sophocles and in defining his concepts he used examples from *Oedipus Tyrannus*. He defined reversal as: 'a change by which the action veers round to its opposite, subject always to our rule of probability or necessity. Thus in the Oedipus, the messenger comes to cheer Oedipus and free him from his alarms about his mother, but by revealing who he is, he produces the opposite effect' (Butcher, 1951, XI 4, p. 41).

He defined recognition as:

A change from ignorance to knowledge, producing love or hate between the persons destined by the poet for good or bad fortune. The best form of recognition is coincident with a Reversal of the Situation, as in Oedipus . . . This recognition combined with Reversal, will produce either pity or fear; and actions producing these effects are those which, by our definition, Tragedy represents (Butcher, 1951, XI 4, 3–4, p. 41).

At the end of his two definitions Aristotle added a very short paragraph: 'A third part is the Scene of Suffering. The scene of Suffering is a destructive or painful action, such as death on the stage, bodily agony, wounds and the like (Butcher, 1951, XI 5, 6, p. 43).

The tragic aspect is how precariously our 'good life' (*eudaimonia*), held in such high esteem by the ancient Greeks, can come to harm, and for that reason the concepts of reversal and recognition are so important in a tragedy. Through them we can acquire an understanding of another key concept in the tragedy, *hamartia*, appropriately translated as 'missing the mark', whereby 'practical error can come about through some causes other than viciousness of character and still matter to the value of a life. Tragedy concerns good people who come to grief not through defect of character and wickedness, but through some *hamartia*' (Nussbaum, 1989, p. 382).

From the 'three unities', which became established as the prescriptive guidelines of how to write a tragedy from the moment that the theatre was re-established in European culture during the sixteenth century, Aristotle only ever developed the 'unity of action' while the 'unity of time' and the 'unity of place' are dealt with in a very brief way. The 'unity of time', also referred to as 'Unity of the Day', rests on one passage in the poetics: 'Epic poetry and tragedy differ, again in their length; for tragedy endeavours, as far as possible to confine itself to a single revolution of the sun, or but slightly to exceed this limit, whereas the epic action has no limits of time' (Butcher, 1951, pp. 289–90).

As for the 'unity of place', it is a general comment about the way plays were staged in ancient Greece, but there is no reference about it anywhere in the *Poetics* and 'as a rule of art, it has been deduced by the critics from the Unity of Time' (Butcher, 1951, p. 291).

The importance that the *Poetics* had in the development of European theatre may well appear disproportionate in relation to its modest proportions, never mind the difficulties inherent in understanding some of Aristotle's key concepts, but its importance cannot be overemphasized ever since the book re-surfaced in a Latin translation during the Renaissance, all the way through to Hollywood, television and cyberspace. This is certainly baffling, but one of the reasons may well be the fact that Aristotle provided critical criteria as useful guidelines of how to produce a good play in which he gave priority to the plot and, among them, gave the famous 'three unities' pride of place. But the irony is that Aristotle was in fact never prescriptive; he merely made suggestions which later became normative criteria for excellence, so that the poor playwrights were constrained to follow them at the expense of freedom of creativity, and this was particularly true in France during the seventeenth century with the emergence of the first professional theatre companies.

In 1498 the Florentine humanist Lorenzo Valla (1407–57) translated the *Poetics* into Latin, and as a consequence Aristotle's ideas, especially 'the three unities', were not only adopted, but became the recognized canon for good playwriting practice. During the Middle Ages, classical theatre disappeared and was replaced by religious street festivals and mystery plays, only to re-emerge during the Renaissance when street spectacle continued to flourish in the form of *commedia del'arte*. Alongside, we witness a revival of interest in Greek and Roman tragedies and comedies under the aristocratic patronage of the Italian princes. Roman playwrights such as Terence, Plautus and Seneca alongside the Greeks – Aeschylus, Sophocles and Euripides – were translated into Italian and performed at princely courts, but no playwrights of the stature of William

Shakespeare emerged in Italy, and this may well had something to do with the prescriptive restrictions imposed on them by the two key manuals, namely Horace's book *The Art of Poetry* and Aristotle's *Poetics*, which were adopted for the study of good practice in writing both tragedy and comedy.

During the sixteenth century, Julius Caesar Scaliger and Ludovico Castelvetro published their commentaries on Aristotle and the *Poetics*, convincing the Renaissance playwrights and public alike to accept 'the three unities', 'as *rules* deduced from classical authority which were to be regarded as binding by dramatists, present and future, and whether composing comedies or tragedies' (Wickham, 1994, p. 101).

Aristotle was particularly influential in the development of French professional theatre during the seventeenth century with the emergence of the first professional actors led by the actor-manager Valleran-Lecomte, who started their existence in a playhouse located in the former palace of the Dukes of Burgundy, the Hôtel de Bourgogne, leased to them by the religious guild of the Confraternity of the Passion, which subsequently became the famed Comédie Française (Wickham, 1994, p. 146):

> This was a long narrow room – Paris never had unroofed theatres like those of London and Madrid – with a platform-stage at one end. In front of it was a pit for standing spectators only, extending back to tiers of rising benches, with boxes at the side. Both stage and auditorium were lit by candles, and all the plays were presented in the old fashioned simultaneous settings which can be seen in the designs by Mahelot, stage-designer for Vallern-Lecomte's company (Hartnoll, 1989, p. 100).

French professional theatre culminated with 'the great quartet': Pierre Corneille, Jean-Baptiste Poquelin (Molière), Jean Racine and Jean-Baptiste Lully (Wickham, 1994, pp. 149–55) and it was with the great tragedy writers Corneille and Racine that there was a return to Aristotle and 'the three unities', which became prescriptive to a fault.

But how did Aristotle's *Poetics* find its way to Hollywood? It is important to notice that Aristotle re-emerged during the twentieth century, but not in the theatre, which continued to evolve during different lines by moving away from creating narratives that imitated human action to other preoccupations: theatre of text, or ideas (Ibsen, Checkhov), epic theatre (Berthold Brecht and Piscator), the theatre of the absurd (Ionesco and Beckett), the theatre of cruelty (Antonin Artaud), poor theatre (Jerzy Grotowski) and then a glorious return to theatre as spectacle during the 1960s with Ariane Mnouchkine and the Théâtre de Soleil, culminating in the 1980s with Peter Brook's awesome epic poem *Mahbharatha*, adopted for the theatre.

Aristotle arrived in Hollywood via the writings of the Russian folklorist Vladimir Propp and those of the American Anthropologist Joseph Campbell, which constituted the starting point for Ari Hiltunen, who became interested in a recurring pattern discussed by Campbell, known as 'the hero's journey', also to be also found in the folktales studied by Vladimir Propp in the early twentieth century. The Hollywood writer Christopher Vogler, who was involved professionally in films such as *The Lion King* and *Beauty and the Beast*, identified the underlining ancient patterns discussed by Campbell and Propp and saw a connection between them and many of the successful movies. Hiltunen then went on to identify the 'proper pleasure' to be found in successful Hollywood blockbusters, such as for instance *The Fugitive* (1993), which took $184 million at the US box office, and after a very long and involved analysis he concluded that the film creates an intense state of undeserved suffering and ends by achieving moral justice. It has several combinations of *'peripeteia and anagnorisis'*. Finally the events 'occur by necessity or probability as Aristotle demanded. The logic of the chain of events makes the story credible and brings about the audience's involvement through the emotions of pity and fear' (Hiltunen, 2002, p. 53). Ari Hiltunen concluded: 'At the dawn of the new millennium, we are entering a new world of stories and, paradoxically, advanced technology is making this transformation from the Information Society even faster. The rulers of this new world will be those who know how to tell great stories' (Hiltunen, 2002, p. 133).

It is an optimistic conclusion, which tells us that essentially what makes us human is unchanging, and that is the ability to tell a good story.

3
TALKING IN PRIVATE: THE ACADEMIES AND THE SALONS

For pity's sake, leave something to my imagination.

Denis Diderot on the painting of François Boucher

At the point of its inception in 1648, L'Académie royale de peinture et de sculpture (in France) was not open to the public. The role of the academy was to teach the precepts of good painting. However, this changed during the eighteenth century when it opened its doors to all, thus providing a public space for intellectual debate concerning the arts. A need was created for an intermediary to explain to the public what the paintings meant, and this was fulfilled by the development of a new profession, that of the critic. Denis Diderot was the first man to fulfil this function. At this point, we will analyse his critical texts and reviews to see how he approached the function of the critic.

In England, in 1768 the Royal Academy of Painting and Sculpture was founded by George III with Sir Joshua Reynolds as its first president. Each year he gave a public lecture providing critical criteria concerning a good practice of painting; his celebrated *Discourses* (from 1769 onwards) were subsequently published. The risk to the artist of depicting contemporary fashions was important to his arguments. William Hogarth's famous engraving *The Analysis of Beauty* (1753) had also revealed the pretentions of fashion by sarcastically commenting on the alleged beauty of new silhouettes. Similarly, *The Five Orders of Periwigs as they were Worn at the Late Coronation Measured Architectonically* (1761) mocked neo-classical meritriciousness and the circle of Lord Burlington. Criticism as an emerging tool therefore began to be applied to fashion in complex ways, and was widely discussed by the educated classes.

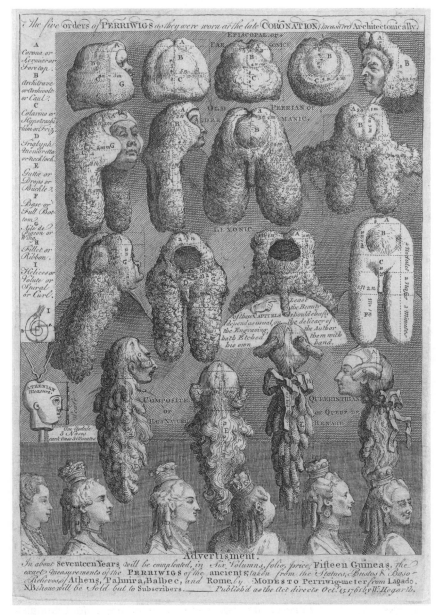

Figure 1 William Hogarth, *The Five Orders of Periwigs as they were Worn at the Late Coronation Measured Architectonically*, 1761, etching and engraving, third of three states, 30.2 × 22.3 cm (plate), National Gallery of Victoria, Melbourne, presented through The Art Foundation of Victoria by Professor P.W. Musgrave, 1995.

Magazines: barometers of taste

Since the emergence in France of the *Mercure Galant* in the reign of Louis XIV, magazines have been mirrors of their times. They not only documented fashions but became barometers of taste. The seventeenth-century magazines had a commercial and publicity remit and tended to describe trimmings and textiles more carefully than the overall 'form' of fashions (Jones, 2004, p. 27), although the silhouette was undoubtedly clear. This changed in the eighteenth century when fashion magazines engaged with the new notion of 'taste' and acquired a higher status and a wider intellectual profile (Miller, 2013, 13–21). By the end of the eighteenth century, about fifteen different fashion journals were printed in England, France, Holland, Germany and Italy, many also showing details of seasonal changes in interior decoration, object and even carriage design.

Journals explicitly directed at women are not numerous in the seventeenth century. They include the English journal *Athenian Gazette* (note the title in light of our Chapter 1) published from 1690, which the editor John Duncton addressed to a female readership, followed by *Ladies Mercury* from 1693 (Van Dijk, 1981, p. 165). The *Mercure Galant* has been considered by Evelyne Sullerot as 'an ancestor of the feminine journal', and the various *Spectators* 'were much read by women' (author's translation of Van Dijk, 1981, p. 165). Scholar of French culture Suzanne Van Dijk argues that many of the journals addressed women's desire to avoid boredom (*ennui*) and uniformity, and encouraged them to embrace 'variety', a thoroughly eighteenth-century obsession. This language of 'variety' for women passed directly into nineteenth- and twentieth-century women's fashion magazines.

Van Dijk noted that fashion journals differentiated themselves from the others (Van Dijk, 1981, p. 166) because they were designed to capture actuality and to inform. However, the matter of amusement remained central; for example, the *Courier de la Mode*, established in 1768 by Boudier de Villemert, was announced in 1770 as joining the ranks of works to amuse. The *Cabinet des Modes*, much imitated and counterfeited abroad, became a great success, augmenting after one year its regularity to three times per month instead of two, and changing its name to *Magasin des Modes Nouvelles Françaises et Anglaises*, allowing a pictorial and a rhetorical dialogue to take place on the page, and inserting both countries into a cosmopolitan circuit of ideas and of exchange. Van Dijk surmised that this change probably resulted from a collaboration with the English publication *Fashionable Magazine*.

Many of the writers of the new fashion journalism of the eighteenth century were women: mesdames de Beaumer, de Maisonneuve and de Princen were journalists at *Journal des Dames*; Madame de Saint-Aubin was at the *Courier de la Nouveauté*; and Madame Dufresnoy was the author of *Courier lyrique et amusant* (Van Dijk, 1981, p. 171).

Understanding taste

Why the focus on taste? The emergence of the concept of 'taste' in eighteenth-century philosophical aesthetics can be observed in the writings of the two main British empirical philosophers of the Enlightenment: Edmund Burke in *A Philosophical Enquiry Into the Origin of Our Ideas of the Sublime and the Beautiful* (1757) and David Hume in *Of the Standard of Taste* (1757). The specialized fashion press first emerged in France shortly afterwards in the 1760s with the publication of *Le Journale de la mode et du Goût* and here we see the definite linking of the concept of taste with fashion. Consisting of detailed texts and copious images, the fashion press published illustrations of breathtakingly varied dress with seasonal and temporal variants. This connection of fashion and taste in the titles of such works has been little remarked on, but it is key to understanding how fashion began to be written about. The development of a periodical press and the related fashion engraving, often hand-coloured, permitted the rapid dissemination of fashionable ideals and spread the cult of individualism, novelty and self-fashioning. A place was found for the new woman reader who was often addressed by and through the concept of fashion. The ideals established in the age of the Enlightenment fashion revolution were long lasting.

The founding of the academies

The founding of the first French academy of painting and sculpture took place during the reign of Louis XIV (1638–1715), nicknamed *le Roi Soleil* (the Sun King), who on the death of his father Louis XIII in 1643 became officially King of France at the age of five. His mother, Queen Anne of Austria, assisted by the first minister of France, Jules, Cardinal Mazarin (1602–61), continued to rule, and only after Mazarin's death in 1661 did Louis XIV effectively become the King of France.

Louis XIV's long reign has been divided into three distinct periods starting with his minority between 1643 and 1661, followed by the most brilliant period of his reign when he embarked on a number of important aesthetic projects, which changed forever the political and cultural face of France as well as its whole society. These included the expansion of the modest hunting lodge his father, Louis XIII, had built at Versailles, which Louis XIV transformed into the most brilliant and celebrated royal residence in the whole of Europe, taking up residence there in 1682. It was only during the third and final period as a king that Louis XIV 'developed into the grim and imposing god-emperor worshipped with complicated ceremonial by a Court of ten thousand people at Versailles' (Wilenski, 1973, p. 70).

One of the King's most important undertakings was the founding in 1648 of the *Académie* royale de peinture et sculpture, but the new institution did not function 'with regular authority' until 1661, when the king's Minister of Finance,

Jean-Baptiste Colbert (1619–83), became its patron (Wilenski, 1973, p. 77). This date marked also the beginning of its pedagogic and artistic activities that transformed 'the trilogy of the Fine Arts', as previously established by the Italian humanist Lorenzo Valla (1406–57). Valla was the first to propose this in his famous text *On the Glory of the Latin Language*, written between 1430–40, which constituted an *oratio* for the glory of Latinity. Having been allowed 'to decay in rust and mould', the Latin language, Valla argued, was in need of being resurrected, as were painting, sculpture and architecture, which he regarded as closest to the liberal arts:

> And many, indeed, and varied are the opinions of wise men on how this happened. I neither accept nor reject any of these daring only to declare soberly that those arts which are most closely related to the liberal arts, the arts of painting, sculpture, modelling, and architecture, had degenerated for so long and so greatly and had almost died with letters themselves, and that in this age they have been aroused and come to life again, so greatly increased is the number of good artists and men of letters who now flourish (Valla in Ross and McLaughlin, 1977, p. 134).

Until the time that Valla was writing, painting, sculpture and architecture were regarded as 'crafts' and therefore belonged to the medieval guild system. They were taught according to the time honoured practice of the apprenticeship system. It comes therefore as no surprise that both Leonardo da Vinci and Michelangelo Buonarotti were apprenticed in the workshops of the sculptor Andrea del Verrochio and the painter Domenico Ghirlandaio respectively, to be trained in the crafts of painting and sculpture. But things were about to change with a group of forward looking Florentine artists, Filippo Brunelleschi, Lorenzo Ghiberti, Donato di Niccolò di Betto Bardi (Donatello) and Tommaso di Ser Giovanni di Simone (Masaccio). Their radical new approach to art was codified by the humanist Leon Battista Alberti (1404–72) in the first theoretical trilogy on the fine arts: *Della Pittura* (1436), *De Re Aedificatoria* (1450) and *De Statua* (1464). In Quattrocento Florence all of the top sculptors were contributing sculptures for the niches on the facade of Or San Michele in order to embellish the streets; it was all public sculpture and not 'gallery art', which is hard now for the public to understand. Good Florentines would have debated in the streets over a good wine whether Ghiberti or Donatello were better.

In his definition of an architect, given in the introduction to his treatise on architecture, Alberti eliminated not only the time honoured definition of all of these arts as crafts (*arti*), which goes back to the ancient Greek concept of *techné* and was referenced in Plato's dialogues, but also to the medieval approach, which regarded them equally as crafts. Alberti rejected all that simply by stating that it is not right to compare an architect with a carpenter:

Before I go any further I think it it will be convenient to say whom exactly I mean to call an architect; for I will not set up before you a carpenter and ask you to regard him as the equal of men deeply versed in the other sciences, though it is true that the man who works with his hands serves as an instrument for the architect (Alberti quoted in Blunt, 1973, p. 10).

What distinguishes the architect from the carpenter is precisely that added dimension that was recognized neither by the ancient Greeks nor during the Middle Ages, namely that his 'craft' was informed by a theoretical framework requiring knowledge which constituted the building blocks on which the first Academy of Fine Arts was opened by Giorgio Vasari in Florence, a century later inspiring Louis XIV and his minister Colbert to follow suit:

I will call an architect one who, with a sure and marvellous reason and rule, knows firstly how to divide things with his mind and intelligence, secondly how rightly to put together in the carrying out of the work all those materials which, by the movements of weights and the conjoining and heaping up of bodies, may serve successfully and with dignity the needs of man. And in carrying out of this task he will have need of the best and most excellent knowledge (Alberti quoted in Blunt, 1973, p. 10).

But it was in his first treatise dedicated to painting that Alberti introduced his analysis of the three theoretical principles, which informed painting as a liberal art rather than 'mere craft':

- his approach to the visible reality peculiarly named *la più grassa Minerva*
- mathematical science as a means of controlling the visual reality *mathematica*
- and most importantly, the story line – that which Aristotle called the plot (*mythos*) – *istoria*, which constituted the key element in a painting (Spencer, 1970, p. 18).

Alberti introduced the concept of *istoria* in Book II of the treatise as 'the greatest work of the painter' because 'it gives greater renown to the intellect than any colossus' (Alberti in Spencer, 1970, p. 72). He was also very specific about the way a painting – whose primary job is to give pleasure – must go about creating such an *istoria*, which in the first instance must be a diverse composition:

The *istoria* which merits both praise and admiration will be so agreeably and pleasantly attractive that it will capture the eye of whatever learned or unlearned person is looking at it and will move his soul. That which first gives pleasure in the *istoria* comes from copiousness and variety of things (Alberti in Spencer, 1970, p. 75).

In the aftermath of the Sack of Rome in 1527, a new period replaced the glorious but short lived 'High Renaissance', Mannerism. Unlike the periods preceding it, Mannerism was an artificially created movement informed by the 'style' called *maniera*, rather than historical considerations with specific guidelines which rejected previous practices. Among the most important was the Albertian definition of a painting as an open window into a reality based on imitation of nature (borrowed from the classical Greek concept of *mimesis*), which was replaced by *maniera*, no longer based on *mimesis* but on a mental construction or invention (*inventione*). Mannerism was born in Florence with the late art of Michelangelo and the mean and moody compositions of Rosso Fiorentino, Andrea del Sarto, Agnolo Bronzino and Domenico Beccafumi, the new generation of artists whom Giorgio Vasari (1511–74) regarded as embodying the highest level of excellence reached by Renaissance artists during the own time.

In 1550 Vasari completed his text *Le Vite dei più ecellenti pittori, scultori é architetti*, dedicated to his patron, Duke Cosimo I Medici, which was reprinted in 1568. In the preface to the second edition, Vasari outlined his aims and objectives behind his decision to undertake the momentous task, which resulted in the birth of the discipline of art history. To that end he intended to leave to posterity the names of the sculptors, painters and architects whose achievements he valued:

In honour of those who are already dead and for the benefit of all scholars, especially those students of the three most excellent crafts of architecture, sculpture and painting, I shall undertake to write the lives of the practitioners of each of them and according to the times during which they lived, one by one, from Cimabue, to date (Vasari, 1997, p. 31).

It was also due to Vasari's enthusiasm that the first Academy of Fine Arts was inaugurated in Florence, and in its statutes presented by Vasari to Cosimo I he stipulated that thirty-three artists – to be selected by Cosimo himself from a list compiled by Vasari – would be appointed to teach the arts. In the decree that followed in 1571, Cosimo exempted the painters and sculptors selected to teach at the Academy from membership of their respective guilds of Arte dei medici é speciali and Arte dei fabbricanti e *Legnaili* (Bazin, 1986, p. 35). This was a turning point in the history of artistic practice and prestige. The Accademia di San Luca inaugurated in Rome in 1593 was even more a teaching institution, more like a kind of 'university for the arts' than its Florentine counterpart, and this was followed in 1598 by the Accademia degli Incaminati founded in Bologna by Ludovico Caracci (Bazin, 1986, p. 35). The radical Italian principle established by the new academic system of teaching and learning ran according to the model that the theoretical study of the liberal arts, including painting, sculpture and architecture, should be taught by the academies, while the mechanical arts should be left to the traditional system of the guilds. This was subsequently adopted in France, and Louis XIV's minister Colbert took it on himself to organize a new system of teaching the arts in France based on this platform. Such a beaux-arts tradition dominated art training around the world for centuries and explains why, for example, in Geneva today, the purpose-built early-twentieth century art schools were on separate sites that were divided into 'fine' and 'applied' art (arts appliqués) with their own buildings with their own conventions and curricula. They have been united only in the past ten years, and where 'fashion design' or the 'fashion arts' as an 'applied' or conceptual art fits into all of this is a conundrum and sometimes also a battle-ground for educators, which impacts the way many students study fashion to the present day.

The Academy of Fine Arts was not the first to be founded in France, as an earlier literary academy had already been inaugurated in 1635, whose aims and objectives was to 'establish the true doctrine in the field of literature' (Blunt, 1991, p. 324), followed by the founding of the Royal Academy of Painting and Sculpture, whose initial function was to exempt artists from membership of the guilds and establish its new approach to teaching, based on theoretical principles rather than practice. In 1663, under the guidance of Colbert, however, its structure was radically altered and a new director appointed, the painter Charles Lebrun (1619–90). As a consequence, the Academy was 'turned into another part of the State art-machine' whereby a rigid teaching hierarchy was established and teaching was carried out accordingly (Blunt, 1991, p. 324).

Colbert, who like so many politicians today was clueless about the arts, regarded them as a convenient vehicle for royal propaganda, and he envisaged them created to celebrate the glory of Louis XIV and indirectly that of France. Having founded the Academy of Painting and Sculpture he proceeded with a host of others: the Royal Academy of Music with Jean-Baptiste Lully (1632–87) as its director, the Royal Academy of Architecture, the Royal Academy of Science and the Royal Academy of Inscriptions. Colbert even envisaged an Académie royale de spectacles to incorporate games, parades, hunting and fireworks (Wilenski, 1973, p. 80). Had he managed to found such an academy, it would have constituted a worthy predecessor of the present UK Ministry of Culture, Media and Sport (DCMS) where the word 'art' does not even figure in the title, reflecting the disregard with which it is treated. It is then not surprising that fashion designers and industry players frequently bemoan the lack of government support for their practice, when not even the hallowed tradition of support of the arts generally is considered obligatory in many contemporary first-world nations.

Lebrun's most important achievement three hundred years ago was to provide a system of quantifying artistic worth. To that end he instructed Henri Testelin

(1616–95) to draw up his synoptic tables of 'Rules for the Great Art' and thus the *Table de Précepts*, for which he selected six artists to be used as canons of excellence on which judgement of good practice were to be based: Le Brun, Michelangelo, Rubens, Poussin, Titian and Rembrandt; their performance were marked between 0 and 18, to be assessed under four headings: composition, drawing, colour and expression (Wilenski, 1973, p. 82). Elsewhere, six headings or 'parts' are listed: line, design, expression, proportion, *chiaroscuro, ordonnance* and colour (Harrison, Wood, Gaiger, 2000, p. 138), further divided into subsections, which constituted the headings under which the artists' artistic worth was judged. For each of the individual 'parts' there would be an explanatory text defining the meaning and usefulness of that particular heading.

Thus the *Third Table of the Precepts in Painting: About Expression* starts with the definition of expression as 'a Representation of things after their nature', which should be considered 'in reference to, A) the subject in general and B) the particular Affections and Passion' (Harrison, Wood, Gaiger, 2000, pp. 139–43). In the section regarding 'affections and passions' the seminal link between 'soul body' is made whereby 'we may express the Passions of the Soul by the actions of the Body, 'tis in the Face nevertheless which man more particularly discern them, by the shape of the Eye, and motion of the Eye-brows' (Harrison, Wood, Gaiger, 2000, pp. 139–43).

The conférences

As the director of the Academy of Painting and Sculpture, Le Brun set out to secure his position. One of his first achievements was to introduce the celebrated Academy Discourses (*conférences*), which were public lectures attended by professors, students and at times members of the public – inaugurated on 7 May 1677 with a discourse on Raphael's painting *St Michael Triumphing Over the Rebel Angels* (Harrison, Wood, Gaiger, 2000, p. 118). One century later, Sir Joshua Reynolds modelled his own *Discourses*, which he delivered at the Royal Academy in London after its inauguration in 1768, on this French approach. One of Charles Le Brun's seminal lectures was the 'conference on expression', that he is alleged to have presented to the Academy in two sessions in April and May of 1668, repeated ten years later in the presence of Colbert, which testifies to the importance that this subject was accorded (Montagu in Harrison, Wood, Gaiger, 2000, p. 131). In it, Le Brun introduced to his audience his own drawings of the various physiognomies resulting from the specific passions he singled out, such as 'Admiration, Esteem, Veneration, Ravishment, Scorn, Horror, Terror, Simple Love, Desire, Hope, Fear, Jealousy, Hatred, Sorrow, Bodily Pain, Joy, Laughter, Weeping, Anger, Extreme Despair and Rage', in which Le Brun revealed his debt to Descartes' book *Traité des passions de l'âme*.

Descartes' dualism

René Descartes' (1596–1650) radical contribution to philosophy, which made him the 'father' of modern philosophy – apart from the famous '*Cogito ergo sum*', which summed up his attempt to make knowledge indubitable (Ayer in Doney, 1968) – was his dualism, which postulated that body and mind are separate entities but act in unison. He introduced his dualism in the second meditation of his celebrated book *Meditations* – first published in Latin in 1641 and subsequently in French in 1647 under the title *Méditations metaphysiques* – in which the resolution of the famous '*Cogito ergo sum*' is proposed. Descartes wittily postulated the existence of a malevolent demon who attempted to deceive him that he exists, whereas in fact he does not exist, but even if this were possible, he was still left with one certainty, because even if he did not exist, his ruminations about his own ontological status are unmistakable; he thinks!:

> But there is some deceiver, supremely powerful, supremely intelligent, who purposely always deceives me. If he deceives me, then again I undoubtedly exist; let him deceive me as much as he may, he will never bring it about that, at the time of thinking that I am something, I am in fact nothing. Thus I have now weighted all considerations enough and more than enough; and must at length conclude that this proposition 'I am', 'I exist', whenever I utter it or conceive it in my mind, is necessarily true (Descartes, 1969, p. 67).

Once the mind is postulated as an independent entity, Descartes proceeded to define the body, here defined as 'whatever is capable of being bounded by some shape, and comprehended by some place, and of occupying space in such a way that all other bodies are excluded' (Descartes, 1969, p. 68). The mind is – of course – the 'I', 'a conscious being', but Descartes, being Descartes, proceeds by asking the same question: 'what is that "I"?' and he finds the answer thus:

> A being that doubts, understands, asserts, denies, is willing is unwilling; further, that has sense and imagination. These are a good many properties – if only they all belong to me. But how can they fail to? Am I not the very person who is now 'doubting' almost everything; who 'understands' something and 'asserts' this one thing to be true, and 'denies' other things . . . (Descartes, 1969, p. 70).

In the *Meditations*, Descartes did not concern himself with emotions, failing to see that they are an integral part of the reasoning 'I', but he made good use of the mind–body dualism to further investigate 'the passions' of the soul elsewhere, in his treatise *Traité des passions de l'âme* published in 1649, one year before his death at the court of Queen Christina of Sweden. In it he provided a rational explanation of human emotions, a subject that would become popular in the philosophy of the Enlightenment. Descartes and his followers, who included the celebrated philosopher Baruch (Benedict) Spinoza (1632–77), who in his influential book *Ethics* (published after his death) dedicated a chapter to the emotions, were using the word *passions*, which had a different meaning from that of the modern word *emotions*, meaning the passive reception of external stimuli, while emotions are something experienced internally. In his public lecture, Le Brun provided a definition of passion as a 'Motion of the Soul, residing in the Sensitive Part thereof, which makes it pursue that which the Soul thinks for its good, or avoid that which it thinks hurtful to it: And for the most part, whatsoever causes Passion in the Soul, makes some Action in the Body' (Harrison, Wood, Gaiger, 2000, p. 132).

He then proceeded to divide the passions into two categories, joy, to which the corresponding bodily action is laughter, and sadness, to which the corresponding bodily action is crying, and then proceeded to show how laughter and crying can be visually captured by the artist.

A more comprehensive *Table of Precepts* was compiled at a later date by the diplomat, painter and critic Roger de Piles (1635–1709), whose book on colour, *Dialogue on Colour* (1673), contradicted the academic principle, which proposed the primacy of drawing over colour. Piles suggested that colour as well as light and shade, for which he was the first to translate the Renaissance term *chiaroscuro* and introduce it into French as *claro obscuro*, defined as 'the art of advantageously distributing the lights and shades which ought to appear in a picture, as well for the repose and satisfaction of the eye, as for the effect of the whole together' (Piles in Holt, 1958, p. 181), were equal in importance to drawing.

In 1708 he published the book *The Principles of Painting with a Balance of Painters* (*Cours de peinture par principes avec un balance de peintres*) in which he compiled a list of fifty-seven major artists he had the opportunity to study during his travelling. His synoptic tables were structured after the model provided by Testelin by being divided into the same four headings: composition, drawing, colour and expression, and marked between 0 and 20, which was tantamount to perfection, with 18 as the highest mark awarded. Unlike Testelin, Roger de Piles included one *Quattrocento* artist, the Venetian champion of *colore* Giovanni Bellini, who scored only 14 for colour and 0 for expression (Brusatin, 1986, pp. 103–4). This should come as no surprise, given that during the *Quattrocento* when portraiture re-emerged in painting, initially under the influence of the profile representations of Roman emperors on coins, the idea of presenting a true likeness, never mind penetrating under the skin to uncover the 'soul' by capturing the sitter's emotions, was not yet understood by painters and therefore expression was still an unknown entity. This is corroborated by what is probably the most famous example in the history of art, 'Mona Lisa's smile'. As a consequence, Leonardo da Vinci's experiments in conveying expression engendered a massive speculative literature, which attempted to explain its 'meaning', very important within the history of criticism as we will see in Chapter 6.

Less famous perhaps, but successful in conveying an emotion, is Raphael's portrait of the diplomat and writer Baldesar Castiglione, whose book *The Courtier* became the approved manual for the Italian courtier, and after Elizabeth I's courtier, Sir Thomas Hoby (1530–66), translated it into English in 1561, also that of the English gentleman, which persists today. Raphael captured to perfection the subtle melancholy of his friend's eyes meant to convey the key characteristic of *sprezzatura* (an elegant detachment from the vulgarity of displaying emotions). But neither Leonardo da Vinci nor Raphael benefited from an academic education, and therefore their attempts to capture the 'passions of the soul' were at the most empirical. In fact Giorgio Vasari relates a delightful story – that Leonardo da Vinci organized special entertainments for La Giaconda, in order to keep her smiling: 'Mona Lisa was very beautiful and whilst Lionardo was drawing her portrait he engaged people to play and sing, and jesters to keep her merry, and remove that melancholy which painting usually gives to portraits' (Vasari, 1963, p. 164).

Vasari's fascinating reference to melancholy as a characteristic that informed portraiture certainly indicates an awareness of the relationship between the facial expression and human emotions; it is interesting to speculate whether its pervasive appearance in Renaissance portraits had anything to do with Castiglione's *sprezzatura* as a signifier of nobility that Raphael captured to perfection in his portrait of the writer, or whether it was something to do with the *Zeitgeist* of their troubled times in the aftermath of the Reformation and the Sack of Rome (1527), which gave birth to the most Saturnian of artistic movements, Mannerism, to which Vasari, too, belonged as a painter.

Expression and its visual representation belonged firmly to the seventeenth century, however, and one of the key reasons was to do with scientific advances in psychology, part of which was publication of René Descartes' seminal book, whose importance for the understanding of human emotions and their visual representation in the arts cannot be overemphasized. The two other headings used in Testelin's and Roger de Piles' synoptic tables were drawing and colour. Controversies regarding the primacy of drawing (*disegno*), considered to be the more intellectual and therefore superior form of art, and *colore*, which emerged in Italy during the Renaissance, traced its emergence back to the *Trecento* and the competition between the Florentine Giotto di Bondone, whose approach to painting was dominated by drawing, and the Siennese Duccio di Buoninsegna, whose paintings were dominated by his love of colour, culminating with the famous *paragone* between Michelangelo and Titian as superlative examples of intellectual *disegno* and emotional *colore* respectively. But while Michelangelo is awarded a mean 4 for colour but 17 for drawing, Titian is awarded 18 for colour but a higher mark of 15 for drawing – which makes him the overall winner in the competition – as he scored higher in drawing, not regarded, at least according to Giorgio Vasari, as his strongest point, while Michelangelo only managed a modest 4 in what was generally regarded his weakest point, colour – nor did he score better when it came to expression, for which he got only 6 (Wilenski, 1973).

Assessments of art: towards criticism

Whether such an authoritarian system was really effective with regard to artistic creativity remains a matter of debate, because although Colbert would have

Figure 2 François Boucher, *The Enjoyable Lesson (L'agréable leçon)* 1748, oil on canvas, 92.5 × 78.6 cm, National Gallery of Victoria, Melbourne, Felton Bequest, 1982.

been satisfied with its rational basis, it 'served no other, because fixed standards have no meaning in the case of the activity called art' (Wilenski, 1973, p. 82). Nevertheless, in the writings of the pioneer art critic and reviewer of the *salons*, Denis Diderot, who was invited by his friend Baron Melchior von Grimm to review the *salons* for him, Diderot, who had no template to follow, made good use of the four categories used in the synoptic tables to assess the ability of the artists selected for assessment. Thus he evaluated the artistic worth of the likes of François Boucher, whom he detested, and Jean-Baptiste Greuze, whom he admired, under the four headings used in the synoptic tables: composition, colour, drawing and expression. Hannah Greig's recent work on the eighteenth-century 'beau monde' notes that the London *Morning Post* in 1776 graded women's beauty according to a scale in which points were awarded for categories including 'expression'; this surely refers to the synoptic tables and would have been recognisable also as something of a joke by those 'in the know' (Greig, 2013, p. 168). Consider how we still work within such expressions today in the west whether describing a detail of a modish outfit or the food at an expensive restaurant, but with little understanding of where and why these terms come into our mouths.

Another important accomplishment of Colbert was not only to make the Royal Collection accessible to the Academy and its teacher and students, but also to reorganize and enrich it with new acquisitions, at times acquired not in the most honourable manner. In 1681 Colbert gathered the royal collection dispersed in various palaces in the galleries of the Louvre and this became also the venue for another important institution that emerged alongside the Academy: the famous *salons*.

The salons

Another significant institution that emerged alongside the Academy and the *conférences* was the *salons*. They emerged concomitantly with the founding of the Royal Academy in Paris during the seventeenth century, but it was not until a century later that they acquired the significance of being the most important locus for the meeting of the arts and the public. During the eighteenth century, the *salons* became a regular event held at the Palais de Louvre, annually between 1737 and 1751, and thence biannually until the Revolution (Wilenski, 1973, p. 133). It was during this period that the 'birth of modern art criticism' has been located, pegged on a specific event: 'the discussion of the 1747 Salon by La Font de St. Yenne' (Harrison, Wood, Gaiger, 2000, p. 425).

Etienne La Font de Saint-Yenne (1688–1771) was a courtier and member of the Academy in Lyons. His special knowledge of painting prompted him to write a review of the 1746 *Salon* published during the following year, in which he not only challenged the professional discussions regarding artistic standards hitherto conducted exclusively among the members of the Royal Academy, but also undertook to deplore publicly the falling standards of his contemporaries unfavourably compared with those of the Old Masters. Notwithstanding the controversy he attracted, an important consequence was 'to initiate a pattern of extensive *Salon* reviews by critics independent of the Academy' (Harrison, Wood, Gaiger, 2000, p. 554), among them the *philosophe* Denis Diderot.

The fortunes of the French Royal Academy changed quite dramatically during the Revolution and the first sign of the process of democratization in its aftermath – which aimed also at turning it into a 'people's academy' – was to open the *salons* to everybody. As a consequence the number of paintings on display doubled from three hundred and fifty pictures in 1789 to seven hundred and ninety-four in 1791 (Wilenski, 1973, p. 166). After the execution of the royal family in 1793, the Jacobin Reign of Terror followed between 1793–94, replaced after the execution of Robespierre with the Directory (1795–99). During these troubled times the Louvre became the *Palais National des Arts* and the 1793 *Salon* – which was the only one to open during the 'Reign of Terror' – received 1,400 separate entries. A new departure was also the addition of an introduction to the official catalogue, on this occasion coming from 'Gazat, Minister of the

Figure 3 James Quinn (Australian 1871–1951, worked in England c.1902 to c.1937), after Jacques-Louis David, *Madame Récamier*, c.1895, oil on canvas, 175.2 × 243.8 cm, National Gallery of Victoria, Melbourne, presented by the artist under the terms of the National Gallery of Victoria Travelling Scholarship, 1895.

Interior/Anonymous: preliminary statement to the Official Catalogue of the Salon of 1793' (Harrison, Wood, Gaiger, 2000, p. 720). Its aims and objectives were to remind painters that their mission was to transcend that of pleasing the eye 'by imitation'; instead they had to create an art of propaganda fit for the new regime for which the one style deemed appropriate was classicism.

The revival of the classical style during the Revolution affected not only the fine arts but extended to all other cultural manifestations such as fashion, with the emergence of the *directoire* style, which transcended sartorial fashion to become a way of life, captured by Jacques Louis David (1748–1825) in his masterpiece *Mme Récamier* (1777–1849) painted in 1800. In this celebrated and much copied portrait, not only did David paint the famous Parisian beauty as a Greek goddess bare-footed, unadorned and clad in a *chiton*-like white outfit, but also represented her reclining on a Pompeian style *méridienne* placed centre stage in her sparsely furnished elegant *salon* perfectly complimenting her sparse classical 'look'. A contemporary diarist wrote of it thus:

> the wisdom of our ancestors exceeded that of later ages. They never manacled the limbs or distorted the person[;] their study in cloathing the body was to unite Ease with use as I have observed & Elegance with comfort . . . It is reported that this mode of attire was introduced at Paris by David the Celebrated Painter and that Madame Racamier [sic] the Bankers Lady so much admired for her beauty wore a muslin so fine that it resembled a mist through which even the colour of her skin could be discover'd. This was adopting a still more ancient fashion than that which Seneca speaks of – Horace describes a Roman lady in her silk dress from the isle of Coris [?] so thin that it might be said to be transparent . . . But the present mode is carried to excess (Trusler, c.1791, n.p.).[1]

What makes this painting so special (David never finished and refused to part with it) is that it provided a visual equivalent of the 'life and style' adopted by the new bourgeoisie created by the revolution that replaced the hated *ancien-régime* with all its Rococo *accoutrements*.

One year later, the Académie royale de peinture et sculpture as well as the provincial art academies were abolished and replaced by a Commune générale des arts. The person responsible for implementing the change was none other than Jacques-Louis David. Apart from producing a succession of iconic paintings, starting with *The Death of Marat* painted during 'The Reign of Terror' when he became 'virtually the Art Dictator of the Republic' (Wilenski, 1973, p. 171), ironically perhaps, David became as much appreciated later by the Emperor Napoléon, who appointed him *premier peintre de l'Empereur* and commissioned him to document his ascendance to power, captured in the monumental masterpiece *The Coronation of Napoleon in Notre Dame*, known as *Le Sacre de Napoléon 1er* (Wilenski, 1973, p. 172). In 1795 the Institut National was founded, which included a new Academié de la litterature et des beaux arts, which became eventually the modern Académie des beaux arts (Wilenski, 1973, p. 167), replicated all around the world from Geneva to Stockholm, as indicated previously.

The first great critic: Denis Diderot

Denis Diderot's career as a *salon* critic was the result of the determination of one man: the German journalist and diplomat Friedrich Melchior, Baron von Grimm (1723–1807), who was despatched by his King Frederick II of Prussia to Paris to report on what was going on in its literary and artistic circles, a function eminently fulfilled by his exclusive journal *Corréspondence littéraire, philosophique et critique*. Although circulated in manuscript form, it gained international success. Initially Grimm reviewed the *salons* himself, starting with 1753, but by 1759 Diderot had replaced him (Harrison, Wood, Gaiger, 2000, p. 592).

The career of Denis Diderot (1713–84) was blighted by hostility, starting with his first important book, *Philosophical Thoughts*, published in 1746, which was burnt for its attack on Christian dogma. Worse still, his *The Letter on the Blind*, published in 1749, resulted in imprisonment. In prison he began work on the monumental *Encyclopédie* (published from 1772) on which he collaborated with some of the most distinguished minds of the French Enlightenment such as Voltaire, D'Alembert, Rousseau and Helvetius (Holt, 1958, pp. 310–11).

Between 1759 and 1767 Diderot reviewed the biennial *salon* art event regularly, gradually increasing the text in bulk to the point that the 1767 review became '*un veritable volume*' thirty times the length of the 1759 review (Delon, 2008, p. 16). During the period between 1769 and 1781 he became a less regular contributor, and in 1773 he embarked on a tour of Europe to visit his benefactor Catherine the Great, who invited him to stay in St Petersburg and offered him a pension. On his return to Paris one year later he contributed another review for the 1775 *Salon* with the last one dated 1781 (Harrison,Wood, Gaiger, 2000, p. 602).

Diderot's first review of the 1759 *Salon* was a modest piece of journalism which started with a general refutation of the quality of the work on show: '*Beaucoup de tableau mon ami, beacoup de mauvais tableaux*' [many paintings my friend, many bad paintings] (Delon, 2008, p. 39); but very swiftly he left behind the uncertainties of the novice and proceeded to develop his unique critical style. This may sound unremarkable, but in fact it is, given that Diderot had no template to guide him and therefore had to invent a critical vocabulary appropriate for his new *métier*. Consequently he followed the time honoured practice of purloining existing methodologies from other disciplines and he turned to what he knew best (and was already well theorized): literature and the theatre. This is why we have been emphasizing art forms other than fashion to this point; criticism has always been drawn from other practices than the one that it appears to evaluate. From the former, he borrowed a well-established rhetorical device: *ekphrasis*. In fact in his 1767 *Salon*, Diderot outlined the two different approaches he proposed to use, and he regarded *ekphrasis* as particularly useful for the analysis of landscapes: 'It is a very good method to describe paintings, above all rural landscapes whereby one can approach the composition either from the right or from the left side and then move along the foreground, describing the objects in order they are located in space' (Diderot quoted by Delon, 2008, p. 20).

Diderot outlined the second approach appropriate for figurative paintings in his *Pensées détaches*:

> I start by specifying the subject; then I move on to the main character and move on to the subordinated characters belonging to the same group, then to the other groups related with the main one, letting myself be guided by the way they are linked to each others through expression, through the *dramatis personae*, through draperies, through colour, the distribution of light and shade, accessories and finally through the overall impression of the entire ensemble (Diderot in Delon, 2008, pp. 20–1).

While in the case of his critical analysis of landscape Diderot made good use of *ekphrasis* by describing what the eye saw with such painstaking attention to detail as to border on boredom, in the case of mythological, historical or religious painting, Diderot was specific about his use of the categories introduced in the synoptic tables of the Academy, such as expression, colour, light and shade and 'the overall ensemble', by which he meant 'composition', to critically evaluate the painting.

This is further testified in his 'Notes on Painting', which he intended 'to serve as an appendix' for the extended review of the 1765 *Salon*, which commenced with 'My eccentric thoughts on Drawing' (Harrison, Wood, Gaiger, 2000, p. 608). In it he criticized the method employed by the Academy, of drawing from the model, with which students began their training. He considered it inadequate and he proposed replacing it with another:

> Here, then, is how I would have a school of drawing run. When the student knows how to draw easily from prints and busts, I keep him for two years before the academic model of man and woman. Then I expose to him children, adults, men in the prime of life, old men, subjects of all ages and sexes, taken from all walks of society, in a word all kinds of characters; the subjects will offer themselves in crowds at the door of my academy, if I pay them well – if I am in a slave country, I shall make them come (Diderot in Holt, 1958, p. 315).

Another source that influenced Diderot's preferential treatment for the dramatic *genre* in painting was the theatre, which re-established itself at the core of seventeenth-century artistic life with the tragedies of Corneille and Racine. Central to the canons of good writing that they established were Aristotle's famous 'three unities' we explored in Chapter 2, but whereby he merely suggested them as the best for 'the proper pleasure' during the seventeenth century, they were later transformed into rigid normative criteria. The critical vocabulary that emerged as a consequence provided Diderot with a template regarding narrative painting, and the painter whom he put centre stage in his work for the dramatic pathos of classical tragedies as well as the stories of the Bible was Jean-Baptiste Greuze; for that reason Diderot esteemed him above all other painters.

Diderot evolved his own critical vocabulary by substituting Aristotle's 'three unities' with the four criteria proposed in Testelin's synoptic table as critical criteria to create a good painting. Nevertheless, Diderot projected his own prejudices and preferences in his reviews of the *salons*; one such example is an ungenerous rant against the perceived superficiality of the *genre* of the *fêtes galantes* celebrated in the paintings of Antoine Watteau, Honoré Fragonard or François Boucher, who stood also for the *ancien régime* (old order), which Diderot had little sympathy for. By contrast, Diderot appreciated Greuze's paintings, which told stories about the happiness resulting from the 'simple life' of country folk in rustic interiors, epitomized in the famed *L'Accordée de village* (The Village Bride) dated 1761.

The 1763 *Salon* provides a good example of Diderot's approach to art criticism, revealing a carefully organized structure always starting with a detailed description of the composition, in which *ekphrasis* is put to good use, and then proceeding to his evaluative criteria derived from the way the composition was thought through. Diderot started his review with the artist Louis-Michel van Loo and then proceeded to analyse two paintings by Boucher: a pastoral scene and a religious subject: *The Sleep of the Infant Jesus*, followed by reviews of the paintings of Deshaies, Loutherbourg, Vernet, Chardin and finally Greuze, singled out for Diderot's conspicuously biased approval with the much quoted words '*C'est vraiment là mon homme que ce Greuze*' [it's truly my only man there Greuze] (Diderot in Delon, 2008, p. 90).

That was certainly not the case with François Boucher, whose charming pastoral scene attracted such a venomous diatribe as to be unacceptable to modern critical sensibilities. Diderot started with his standard description of the subject matter:

Imagine in the background a vase on a pedestal crowned with a bunch of heavily drooping branches; beneath it, a shepherd asleep in the lap of his shepherdess. Arrange around them a shepherd's crook, a little hat full of roses, a dog, some sheep, a bit of countryside and countless other objects piled on top of each other. Paint the lot in the brightest colours, and there you have Boucher's *Pastoral Scene* (Harrison, Wood, Gaiger, 2000, p. 603).

So far so good, but what follows amounts to what can be regarded as tantamount with an assassination of Boucher's artistic worth:

What a misuse of talent! How much time gone to waste! You could have had twice the effect for half the effort. With so many details all equally carefully painted, the eye doesn't know where to look. No air. No rest. And yet the shepherdess does have the right face for her station. And this bit of countryside surrounding the vase does have a delicacy, a freshness, a surprising charm. But what does this vase and its pedestal mean? What's the meaning of those heavy branches on top of it? When one writes, does one have to write everything? And when one paints, does one have to paint everything? For pity's sake, leave something to my imagination (Harrison, Wood, Gaiger, 2000, p. 603).

A nod of approval regarding the country landscape, but the rest is simply no good, and here Diderot was specific about Boucher's shortcomings. What is interesting, though, is the importance accorded to the imagination as the faculty central to artistic creativity. Finally, Diderot concluded his review with an invective declaring Boucher to be 'the ruination' of young artists. What could be nastier?:

This man is the ruination of all young apprentice painters. Barely able to handle a brush and hold a palette, they torture themselves stringing together infantile garlands, painting chubby crimson bottoms, and hurl themselves headlong into all kinds of follies which cannot be redeemed by originality, fire, tenderness nor by any magic in their models. For they lack all these (Harrison, Wood, Gaiger, 2000, p. 603).

By contrast Greuze could do no wrong, and Diderot selected the painting entitled *Filial Piety* for his enthusiastic approval. He started in the usual manner with a detailed description of the composition: 'the main figure, occupying centre stage, and who captures our attention, is a paralysed old man, stretched out in his armchair, his head on a pillow and his feet on a stool. He is fully dressed' (Harrison, Wood, Gaiger, 2000, p. 605) and several pages and descriptive details later he brought into discussion all the alleged negative issues raised by the critics with regard to the painting, starting with such an utterly banal observation as 'some say the paralytic is leaning too far back and that it is impossible for him to eat in such a position', for which Diderot – of course – had the answer, 'He is not eating, he is speaking and someone is ready to lift his head for him' (Harrison, Wood, Gaiger, 2000, p. 606). Finally, after a succession of similarly inane comments, Diderot offered his verdict in no uncertain terms: 'That . . . damn those critics and me with them! The painting is beautiful, very beautiful, and woe betide anyone who is able to look at it for a single moment and remain unmoved!' (Harrison, Wood, Gaiger, 2000, p. 606). Diderot went on to list the specific qualities that made Greuze's painting beautiful.

Predicating 'beauty' of itself as a value judgement is very important because it brings us to the emergence during the eighteenth century of the new discipline of philosophical aesthetics and the introduction of its four classical categories: two borrowed from ancient theatre, the tragic and the comic; and two borrowed from philosophy, the ancient Greek concept of beauty, as well as a new one which emerged in British empirical philosophy: the sublime. Predicating 'beauty' of a painting that fulfilled certain characteristics, however, randomly selected by Diderot, nevertheless required an enabling faculty that perceived it to be so: 'Taste', will be discussed next in Chapter 4.

4

UNDERSTANDING TASTE: THE CRITIC AS QUALIFIED OBSERVER

It is natural to seek a *Standard of Taste*; a rule by which the various sentiments of men may be reconciled; at least a decision afforded confirming one sentiment, and condemning another.

David Hume, *Of the Standard of Taste*, 1757

When we make an aesthetic judgement about a thing, we do not just gape at it and say: 'Oh! How marvellous!'. We distinguish between a person who knows what he is talking about and a person who doesn't.

Barrett, 1967, p. 6

Philosophical aesthetics is a branch of philosophy which emerged during the period that we now call the Enlightenment; its main area of inquiry is the concept of 'taste'. The Enlightenment itself is an elusive concept and this is testified to by the wealth of definitions and explanations found in the specialized literature. If we accept the standard dictionary definition of the Enlightenment as 'an 18th century philosophical movement stressing the importance of reason and the critical reappraisal of existing ideas and social institutions' (*Collins English Dictionary*, 2005, p. 545), this provides a useful starting point for the investigation of 'taste' as a concept created by all of these developments.

Defining philosophical aesthetics

Philosophical aesthetics is a branch of philosophy which deals with the aesthetic experience specifically relegated to artistic appreciation, as well as aesthetic judgement and taste as they emerged during the Enlightenment, in the writings of David Hume and Immanuel Kant (Gardner in Grayling, 1995, pp. 585–6). As a movement relegated to intellectual pursuits, it could be argued that the Enlightenment would have had little impact on society and its ills, but nothing is further from the truth, because we are faced with a perfect example of how theory informs practice on a heroic scale, given the Enlightenment's impact on society, starting with the event that changed the face of European history by ushering in Modernism: the French Revolution (1789–99), as repeatedly pointed out in all key areas of scholarship.

Thus the philosopher Jonathan I. Israel started his monumental tome *Enlightenment Contested* by confirming its impact on the French Revolution: 'Even a cursory study of the French Revolution will soon convince an attentive student that the ideology and rhetoric of revolution in late eighteenth-century Europe, and not least the slogans – "liberty", "equality" and "fraternity" – were very intimately connected with the new ideas of the Enlightenment' (Israel, 2008, p. 3)

The mind was thus now the engine of problem solving. The word 'aesthetics' derived from the Greek word *aesthesis*, meaning 'perception', and for the Greeks, it referred to 'perception by means of the senses' (Collinson in Hanfling, 1992, p. 112). In the eighteenth century the philosopher Alexander Gottlieb Baumgarten (1714–62) specifically related the concept to art and beauty, first in the *Meditations* (whose complete title is *Philosophical Meditations on some Matters pertaining to Poetry*) published in Latin in 1735, and then in his unfinished book *Aesthetica*, published in 1750 (Harrison, Wood, Gaiger, 2000, p. 487). Initially the concept was used in relation to sense experience, as when we look at a painting we start with perceiving 'forms, lines, colours, spaces and textures', and only after that do we come to the aesthetic experience and enjoy its 'liveliness or calm, harshness, boldness or serenity, lyricism or wit, joyousness or foreboding' (Collinson in Hanfling, 1992, p. 112).

But things are more complicated when it comes to the origins of the concept of aesthetic experience, which has been traced back to the seventeenth century and the rationalist philosophy of René Descartes (1596–1650), who argued that knowledge cannot be based either on experiment or empirical observation, but is instead based on deductive reasoning and innate (*a priori*) ideas. This 'ideal of Cartesian knowledge' spread across Europe, and 'the hope of attaining it arose in many fields, including the study of the arts' (Beardsley, 1966, 141)

Artistic creativity was reconsidered according to the Cartesian model as being rooted in reason but informed by nature, and therefore reason and nature became the twin foundations on which the critical criteria for the creation of good art were rooted. But while reason may appear self-evident, the introduction of nature needs further elucidation, and the first clues that led to its introduction in critical discourse were traced back to Aristotle's *Poetics*: 'One principle (or definition) was taken as axiomatic: that poetry is an imitation of human action. But this idea had now to be developed and systematized, with the help of the emerging concept of Nature. The clue was taken from the *Poetics*: poetry is universal whereas history is particular' (Beardsley, 1966, p. 143).

Aristotle argued that reason grasps the universal in the particular and his principle of universality was adopted as the basis of neo-classical theory. From the wealth of the examples available, Sir Joshua Reynolds was singled out as the paradigmatic proponent of neo-classicism: 'the basic ideas of neoclassical theory in the fine arts were set forth in definitive form, with clarity and grace and judicious qualification, by Sir Joshua Reynolds, in his *Discourses on Art* (delivered at the English Royal Academy from 1769 to 1790, the first seven published in 1778) (Beardsley, 1966, p. 149).

In his 'Third Discourse', delivered to the students of the Academy on 14 December 1770, Sir Joshua Reynolds discussed the importance of imitation from nature for the good practice of art. He argued that the young painter must acquire technical dexterity first for perfect imitation, but then transcend the 'implicit submission to authority', not to preclude themself 'from the abundance and variety of Nature', nor must nature be slavishly followed: 'I will now add that Nature herself is not to be too closely copied' (Reynolds, 1969, p. 43). The reason given is that 'perfection of this art (painting) does not consist in mere imitation'. At this point he introduced the concept of ideal beauty as the *telos* (final cause) that motivates all artistic creation: 'The poets, orators, and the rhetoricians of antiquity, are continually enforcing this position; that all the arts receive their perfection from an ideal beauty, superior to what is to be found in individual nature' (Reynolds, 1969, pp. 43–4).

Reynolds referenced Plato's idealist view of the transcendental nature of beauty, which can only be experienced as an ideal (universal) form rather than in particulars. 'The Artist is supposed to have ascended the celestial regions, to furnish his mind with this perfect idea of beauty' (Reynolds, 1969, pp. 43–4).

In his ninth, very short, discourse delivered on 16 October 1780, Reynolds defined the aim of painting, which can only be beauty:

The Art which we profess has beauty for its object; this it is our business to discover and to express; but the beauty of which we are in quest is general and intellectual; it is an idea that subsists only in the mind; the sight never beheld it, nor has the hand expressed it: it is an idea residing in the breast of the artist, which he is always labouring to impart, and which he dies at last without impairing; but which he is yet so far able to communicate, as to raise thoughts, and extend themselves imperceptibly into publick [sic] benefits (Reynolds, 1969, p. 151).

Baumgarten's intention was to produce an aesthetic theory which combined two seemingly incompatible notions: Cartesian rationalist knowledge based on deductive principles separated from anything to do with reality (empirical), and perception, which is the way we relate to the outside world through our five senses and how the object of our perception is translated into mental concepts. Baumgarten regarded perception as a 'lower level of cognition' and in that sense he defined aesthetics as 'the science of sensory cognition' (Beardsley, 1966, p. 156). Thus a new theory of aesthetics was proposed, defined simply as a lower level of the Cartesian deductive system of knowledge applied in science but good enough for the confused domain of the arts, and Baumgarten called this 'sensate discourse'; the important point here is that he firmly relegated 'sensate discourse' to rationalist knowledge.

We find these definitions in his 'Prolegomena' to *Aesthetica*, in which he defined aesthetics as 'the theory of the liberal arts, the lower study of perception, the art of thinking in the fine style, the art of analogical reasoning, a science of perception that is acquired by means of the senses' (Baumgarten in Harrison, Wood, Gaiger, 2000, p. 489). Baumgarten also made an important point, regarding the link between aesthetics and criticism; replying to an imaginary objection regarding his new science of aesthetics that could be seen as 'the same thing as criticism', he argued: 'I reply a) there is also critical logic, b) a certain type of criticism is an element of aesthetics, c) for this a previous knowledge of the rest of aesthetics is almost indispensable, if one does not wish to discuss the matter simply on the basis of tastes in judging the excellence of thought, of spoken and written material' (Baumgarten in Harrison, Wood, Gaiger, 2000, p. 49).

Clearly he does not regard criticism and aesthetics as coextensive, because while some types of criticism belong to aesthetics, the new science of 'sensory cognition' is useful for avoiding the type of criticism based solely on taste, which we will find alive and well in British empiricist philosophy.

Aesthetics, beauty and criticism in modern philosophy

Taste, which played a central role in the emergence of philosophical aesthetics, is defined as a special faculty that enables us to discern aesthetic qualities, especially beauty, regarded during the eighteenth century as the most important quality of works of art. Its use in modern and contemporary aesthetics declined and its only use is 'in the broad sense of aesthetic preference' (Cooper, 1995, p. 415). The reason is that if beauty does not reside in the object in the way in which red or rectangular do, then an aesthetic judgement is subjective and therefore can only reference an individual response, and twentieth-century philosophers do not accept that.

As a logical positivist, at least to start with, Sir Alfred Ayer (1910–89) argued in his famous book *Language, Truth and Logic* that aesthetic terms are used in a way similar to ethical ones and words like 'beautiful' and 'hideous' do not report facts but express 'certain feelings and evoke a certain response'. For that reason, 'there is no sense in attributing objective validity to aesthetic judgements, and no possibility of arguing about questions of value in aesthetics, but only about questions of fact'. Ayer further argued that if we could produce a scientific treatment of aesthetics, which we cannot, that would show 'what in general were the causes of aesthetic feeling whereby various societies produced and admired the works of art they did, why taste varies as it does within a given society, and so forth' (Ayer, 1971). These are questions which have nothing to do with aesthetics, as they pertain to psychology or sociology, but nor do they have much to do with aesthetic criticism, as Ayer points out, for a simple reason:

> the purpose of aesthetic criticism is not so much to give knowledge as to communicate emotion. The critic, by calling attention to certain features of the work under review, and expressing his own feelings about them, endeavours to make us share his attitude towards the work as a whole. The only relevant propositions that he formulates are propositions describing the nature of the work. And these are plain records of fact. We conclude, therefore, that there is nothing in aesthetics, any more than there is in ethics, to justify the view that it embodies a unique type of knowledge (Ayer, 1971, p. 15).

It got worse with Ludwig Wittgenstein (1889–1951). In his posthumously published book *Lectures and Conversations on Aesthetics, Psychology and Religious Belief* (1967), he started with what appears self-evident, by arguing that aesthetics:

> is very big and entirely misunderstood as far as I can see. The use of such a word as 'beautiful' is even more apt to be misunderstood if you look at the linguistic form of sentences in which it occurs than most other words. 'Beautiful' (and 'good') is an adjective, so you are inclined to say: 'This has a certain quality, that of being beautiful (Wittgenstein, 1967, p. 1).

He then revisited his often quoted (and much loved by philosophy students) definition of 'family resemblance', introduced first in *Philosophical Investigations*:

> I have often compared language to a tool chest, containing a hammer, chisel, matches, nails, screws, glue. It is not a chance that all these things have been put together – but there are important differences between the different tools – they are used in a family of ways – though nothing could be more different than glue and chisel (Wittgenstein, 1967, p. 1).

The question that led Wittgenstein to a definition of beauty was to ask how does a child learn of it? And the answer was 'through interjections', but then he made the even stranger claim that 'beautiful is an odd word to talk about because it's hardly ever used'. Instead, the child learns first a word such as 'good' (analogous to beautiful), first applied to food, and the word is taught as 'substitute for a facial expression or a gesture. The gestures, tones of voice, etc., in this case are expressions of approval.' What matters is the way language is used, for example not the actual words 'beautiful' or 'good', but the occasions on which they are used, and if their first use was as interjections then it 'would not matter if instead of saying "This is lovely", I just said "Ah!" and rubbed my stomach' (Wittgenstein, 1967, p. 3).

This is not how it is in 'real life', by which Wittgenstein meant twentieth-century philosophy, because aesthetic judgements no longer employ traditional aesthetic categories, such as 'the beautiful', no longer found either in musical or poetic criticism. Instead, we say (Wittgenstein's examples) in the case of the former 'Look at this transition' or 'the passage here is incoherent', or in the latter 'his use of images is precise' and these words are more akin to 'right' and 'correct' (as used in ordinary speech) than to 'beautiful' and 'lovely'. A word such as 'lovely' predicated of music would be first used as interjection: 'We might say of a piece of music that it is lovely, by this not praising it but giving it a character' (Wittgenstein, 1967, p. 3).

Finally we have a kind of definition of what may amount to the qualified observer (the critic) coming from Wittgenstein and for such a person using words like 'beautiful' are simply tantamount to 'ah!!!':

> In what we call the Arts a person who has judgement develops. (A person who has a judgement doesn't mean a person who says 'Marvellous!' at certain things.) If we talk of aesthetic judgements, we think, among a thousand things, of the Arts. When we make an aesthetic judgement about a thing, we do not just gape at it and say: 'Oh! How marvellous!' We distinguish between a person who knows what he is talking about and a person who doesn't (Wittgenstein, 1967, p. 6).

Wittgenstein introduces the critic, the person 'who knows', whom David Hume called two centuries before 'the qualified observer', who alone can explain both the 'psychological causes and effects of works of art'. This was one of the seminal contributions of British empirical philosophy and 'from their discoveries, or seeming discoveries, about such processes as creative imagination and aesthetic enjoyment, the empiricist aestheticians drew many conclusions of considerable – historical – and some of permanent – significance' (Beardsley, 1966, p. 167).

British empiricism and its contribution to philosophical aesthetics

In complete opposition to European rationalism, British empiricist philosophy considers that all knowledge is ultimately derived from experience. As cogently summed up by A.C. Grayling:

> The paradigm of knowledge for rationalist is accordingly the formal deductive system, like geometry or logic, where excogitation from first principles, self-evident truths, or definitions leads to bodies of wholly certain knowledge. Empiricists, by contrast argue that knowledge cannot come from an armchair speculation, but only from going and looking. Use of our senses (and instruments that extend their range) can alone inform us about contingent matters of fact (Grayling, 1995, p. 486).

The Enlightenment is regarded as the result of the twin developments of the European rationalist philosophy of René Descartes, Baruch Spinoza (1632–77) and Gottfried Wilhelm Leibniz (1646–1716) and the British empiricists, John Locke (1632–1704), George Berkeley (1685–1753) and David Hume (1711–76).

In his 'Discourse on Method' (1637), Descartes proposed a new theory of knowledge based on a systematic process of doubt (scepticism), which led to the famous 'I think therefore I am' (Honour and Fleming, 1982, p. 426), while the empiricists introduced their own methodology borrowed from science: the inductive method first introduced by Francis Bacon (1561–1626), which starts from the particular observation (a scientific experiment) and after repeated confirmations becomes universal law, as a reverse of the Aristotelian deductive system, which starts from an unverified hypothesis and through a sequence of logical steps arrives at a necessarily true conclusion: 'As Descartes, no doubt with some arbitrariness, is often placed at the fountainhead of modern rationalism, so Sir Francis Bacon, with perhaps less solid claim, is generally regarded as the first mover, or at least the herald and pilot projector of modern empiricism' (Beardsley, 1966, p. 167).

With regard to philosophical aesthetics, the rationalist approach is also distinct from that of the empiricists; while the former target the work of art (the object), the latter are concerned with the psychological effects (the subject), reverting in a way to Aristotle's concern with the way the 'proper pleasure' (*oikeia hedone*) of a well-written tragedy results in purgation (catharsis):

> Neoclassical rationalism and formalism . . . claimed to derive its logical force from the analysis of the essential nature of the arts . . . The Baconian tradition, on the other hand, called attention from the start to the need for empirical

study of the psychological processes involved in art, and in the seventeenth and eighteenth centuries the British school concentrated its main, and most fruitful effort on this task (Beardsley, 1966, p. 167).

The first concept regarded as an important vehicle to facilitate the aesthetic experience is the concept of the imagination, which for the rationalists had little value because of its low epistemological content, but it attracted the empiricists starting with Francis Bacon, who defined poetry as 'feigned history', whose function was to 'give some shadow of satisfaction to the mind of man in those points wherein the nature of things doth deny it' (Beardsley, 1966, p. 170). Its first proper definition can be found in *Leviathan* by Thomas Hobbes (1588–1679), first published in 1651. In Part I, entitled 'Of Man', Chapter 2 is dedicated to the imagination, charmingly defined as 'decaying sense':

> For after the object is removed, or the eye shut, we still retain an image of the thing seen, though more obscure than when we see it. And this is it, the Latines call *Imagination* from the image made in seeing . . . but the Greeks call it *Fancy*; which signifies *appearance*, and is as proper to one sense, as to another. IMAGINATION therefore is nothing but *decaying sense* (Hobbes, 1985, p. 88).

Hobbes further divided imagination into simple and compounded. Simple imagination is 'when one imagineth a man, or horse, which he hath seen before' while compound imagination is defined as 'when from the sight of a man at one time, and of a horse at another, we conceive in our mind a Centaure' (Hobbes, 1985, p. 89).

It is in its second form that imagination emerges as the creative faculty placed centre stage in critical discourse. Thus in his vitriolic review of François Boucher for the *Salon of 1763* – referred to in the previous chapter – Denis Diderot deplored artists' tendency in literature and painting towards *horror vacui*, to the detriment of creativity: 'When one writes, does one have to write everything? And when one paints, does one have to paint everything? For pity's sake, leave something to my imagination' (Diderot in Harrison, Wood, Gaiger, 2000, p. 603).

Defining taste: the Earl of Shaftesbury, David Hume and Edmund Burke

The concept of taste, in the sense of our ability to discern the qualitative attributes of a work of art 'X', which confer on it artistic worth, not only preoccupied artists, theoreticians and philosophers, but expanded into the 'lesser' realms of journalism and the everyday, including clothes, furniture, domestic interiors, or 'life/style' as we call it today. Not surprisingly, we find taste incorporated in titles of numerous eighteenth- and nineteenth-century fashion magazines. The question is whether it is simply meant as a discerning ability to wear what was 'in fashion' and therefore considered 'tasteful', or whether it preserved its philosophical and theoretical implications when applied to fashion. This question will, we hope, be answered after presenting a historical overview of taste as used in eighteenth-century British empiricism, starting with the pioneering writings of the Earl of Shaftesbury.

The Earl of Shaftesbury

Anthony Ashley Cooper, 3rd Earl of Shaftesbury (1671–1713), addressed three important issues which take centre stage in the writings of his followers, including Immanuel Kant, the most important being 'taste'. Shaftesbury introduced the curious notion of 'the inward eye', a faculty that doubled in evaluating human actions (ethics) as well as beauty (aesthetics). Thus beauty and goodness are identical and grasped by the same faculty of the 'inward eye': 'The theory of this "inward eye", to which Shaftesbury gave the name "moral sense", was his contribution to eighteenth-century ethical theory, and at the same time to aesthetics. For the faculty that is called a moral sense when applied to human actions and dispositions is the sense of beauty when applied to external objects, of nature or Art' (Beardsley, 1966, p. 179).

However, his followers Addison, Hutchinson, Hume and Burke separated ethics from aesthetics using the concept of 'taste' exclusively as the faculty applicable to the arts. This distinction culminated in Immanuel Kant's trilogy of critical philosophy, in which he developed his transcendental idealism: *Critique of Pure Reason* (1781), *Critique of Practical Reason* (1788) and *Critique of Judgement* (1790). In the last volume, dedicated to aesthetics, Kant stated that the aesthetic experience cannot be understood without relating to our moral nature and therefore the beautiful must be considered as the symbol of the morally good. Thus we come back full circle to Shaftesbury's 'inward eye', the only difference being Kant's modern terminology.

Two more concepts pioneered by Shaftesbury are the notion of 'disinterestedness', which again will be developed by Kant into one of the four partial definitions of the concept of beauty, and the 'sublime', to which Kant devoted half of the text of *Critique of Judgement*, the other half being beauty. The enjoyment of beauty must be free of interest in the sense of being free of practical interest such as the desire, in the case of the visual arts, to possess the work of art.

The sublime

One of Shaftesbury's most enduring contributions to aesthetics was the postulation of the new aesthetic category of the sublime, specifically relegated to nature. The sublime was not entirely an eighteenth-century invention; we can trace it to the writings of the treatise *On the Sublime* (Peri Hypsous), allegedly written by a mysterious Longinus of Emesa (c. AD 213–73), the minister of Queen Zenobia of Palmyra, but in fact we do not know its author's real identity.

The treatise achieved popularity during the eighteenth century in literary criticism starting with the translation by Nicolas Boileau (1636–1711) in 1674, whereby the sublime is relegated to the lofty or elevated style of writing. However, this is not the sense in which the sublime was used by either Shaftesbury or his followers, who relegated it to nature as a subject of aesthetic contemplation that resulted in the experience of the sublime in the contemplation of nature in all its grandeur, which contains intimations of infinity and ultimately of God.

Before proceeding to discuss David Hume, two important precursors, Joseph Addison and Francis Hutchenson, deserve a mention. Joseph Addison (1672–1719) can be regarded as the father of enlightened journalism (Mackie, 1997). He was a founder, together with Richard Steele of *The Tatler* (1709–11) and *The Spectator* (1711–12 and 1714), both short lived but popular intellectual periodicals (now 'magazines') favoured in the coffee houses of London. For the latter Addison contributed a series of articles he called 'papers', under the title 'The Pleasures of the Imagination', which established him as the 'premier arbiter of taste' (Harrison, Wood, Gaiger, 2000, p. 382) in England. Visibly under the influence of Thomas Hobbes, he regarded sight as the most important of our senses and he defined the imagination in Paper 1 (21 June 1711) as something located between the senses and the mind:

> It is this sense (sight) which furnishes the imagination with its ideas; so that by 'the pleasures of the imagination' or 'fancy' (which I shall use promiscuously), I here mean such as arise from visible objects, either when we have them actually in our view, or when we call up their ideas into our minds by painting, statues, descriptions, or any the like occasion (Harrison, Wood, Gaiger, 2000, p. 382).

In his second paper (23 June 1711), Addison explained the importance of the imagination in our experience of beauty:

> But there is nothing that makes its way more directly to the soul than beauty, which immediately diffuses a secret satisfaction and complacency through the imagination, and gives a finishing to any thing that is great or uncommon. The very first discovery of it strikes the mind with an inward joy, and spreads

a cheerfulness and delight through all its faculties (Addison in Harrison, Wood, Gaiger, 2000, p. 385).

Interestingly, Addison introduced the two different kinds of beauty properly developed by Edmund Burke – who is reported to have read *The Spectator* in 1744 when he was a student at Trinity College, Dublin – and was particularly influenced by Addison's *The Pleasures of the Imagination*. The first beauty is that of the species: 'Thus we see that every different species of sensible creatures has its different notions of beauty, and that each of them is most affected with the beauties of its own kind', but Addison warned, this is no more remarkable than 'in birds' (Harrison, Wood, Gaiger, 2000, p. 385). Burke developed a much more complex debate, by introducing the 'passions which belong to society' further distinguishing 'the society of the sexes' from 'general society', the latter strictly to do with sex. Here Burke contradicted Addison: 'But this preference, I imagine, does not arise from any sense of beauty which they find in their species, as Mr Addison supposes, but from a law of some other kind to which they are subject (Burke, 1990, p. 39). That law presupposes an additional 'social' quality which adds to the attraction of the sexes over and above the animal realm, because it is determined by society, and that he called 'the beauty of the sex', whereby 'Men are carried to the sex in general, as it is the sex, and by the common law of nature, but they are attached to particulars by personal beauty. I call beauty a social quality' (Burke, 1990, p. 39).

Addison's second beauty is more relevant to this debate, as he predicated it of arts and nature, which 'does not work in the imagination with that warmth and violence as the beauty that appears in our proper species, but it is apt however to raise in us a secret delight, and a kind of fondness for the places or objects in which we discover it'. Addison provided the usual list of colours, and symmetry and proportion in parts, arrangement and disposition of the bodies to do with the arts as well as what we see in nature, such as 'the rising and setting of the sun (Harrison, Wood, Gaiger, 2000, p. 385).

Francis Hutcheson's philosophical aesthetics

Francis Hutcheson (1694–1746) is generally accepted to be the author of the first modern book on philosophical aesthetics, entitled *An Inquiry concerning Beauty, Order, Harmony and Design*, which formed the first half of *An Inquiry into the Original of our Ideas of Beauty and Virtue*, published in 1725. Central to his inquiry is the question: 'What is the source of the pleasure we take in beauty?', and for that he has the same two answers, which in one way or another inform the main concerns of eighteenth-century philosophical aesthetics.

The answer is twofold: the source of pleasure we get from beauty lies within us and also with the object, in other words an objective and a subjective dimension put together. By 'within us' Hutcheson makes it clear that it has nothing to do with reason in the sense of not pertaining to 'rational' pleasures. He postulates a new category, 'internally sensible':

> the pleasure of beauty cannot arise with the involvement of reason, and therefore must have its source solely in the senses and . . . the pleasure of beauty cannot arise solely from external sources, and therefore can arise only with the involvement of some internal source . . . By establishing these two points, Hutcheson forces the acknowledgment of a new category of pleasures: to the (externally) sensible and the (internally) rational, we must add the internally sensible, a category consisting of those pleasure that arise only with the involvement of some internal sense, which includes the pleasure of beauty (Shelley in Gaut and Lopes, 2001, p. 39).

Accepting Hutcheson's argument that the pleasure of beauty does not involve reason poses complications given that he proposed a very specific quality, that of 'uniformity amidst variety' that an object must possess in order to produce in us the pleasure of beauty. We would need our rational faculties to work this out and for that reason David Hume rejected Hutcheson's argument, reinstating reason within the aesthetic experience.

Hume's fork

David Hume is best known for his formidable contributions to epistemology, political theory and morality, which he developed in his two key books: *A Treatise of Human Nature*, published in 1739 when he was not thirty, yet whose failure was famously summed up by him with the words 'it fell dead born from the press', followed by his *magnum opus* entitled *An Enquiry Concerning Human Understanding*, published in 1748, in which we find – among other arguments – the most famous refutation of metaphysics so beloved by philosophy students, known as 'Hume's fork', with which Hume demolished metaphysics with a stroke as worthless, because it does not belong either to analytical or empirical knowledge:

> When we run over libraries, persuaded of these principles, what havoc must we make? If we take in our hand any volume; of divinity or school metaphysics, for instance; let us ask, Does it contain any abstract reasoning concerning quantity or number? No. Does it contain any experimental reasoning concerning matter of fact and existence? No. Commit it then to the flames; For it can contain nothing but sophistry and illusion (Hume, 1977, p. 785).

Nevertheless, Hume's attention was attracted by the concept of taste, and in 1757 he published his collection of essays *Of the Standard of Taste*, the same year that his younger contemporary Edmund Burke (1729–97) published *A Philosophical Enquiry into the Origin of our Ideas of the Sublime and Beautiful*. Finally moving away from empiricism, *Critique of Judgement* by Immanuel Kant (1724–1804) revisited the concept of taste. What was the reason for the popularity of the concept of 'taste', starting with the high echelons of philosophy and then 'trickling down' to lesser intellectual fields of inquiry including the fashion periodical, as mentioned earlier?

It would not be possible to provide one answer, but some of the reasons which contributed to creating the 'eighteenth-century mind' include the strange mixture of deference and squalor which typified life in an eighteenth-century town or city. Against this maddeningly complex background, taste dominated artistic discourse, in turn rooted in philosophical discourse, class and social hierarchy, but in the aftermath of the French Revolution, the process of democratization which manifested itself at an intellectual level with the famous *querelle* (argument) between the ancients and moderns became not only democratized but also, yes, 'popularized'. This is reflected in the newly emergent fashion magazines, which introduced the lofty concept of taste into the everyday, whose aims and objectives were not so much to make accessible aesthetic concepts such as beauty and the sublime – that was the job of Joseph Addison and his column for *The Spectator* – rather the issues revolved around deciding which latest millinery or head-dress was in the 'best possible taste' for such and such a time of the day, or what choice of window hanging must a hostess 'of taste' choose for an 'elegant' (*de bon ton*; in good taste) residence. Amusing periodicals with names such as *Bon Ton Magazine: or Microscope of Fashion and Folly* included illustrations such as 'Critical Observations upon Beauty' (1795), which were spoofs on the contemporary interest in debating taste and aesthetics, even Plato's cave, back-lit projections, classical scenes of erotic love and a cuckolded husband.

Hume started his essay in a chatty manner, by asking whether it is possible at all – given the variety of taste to do with human nature – to have a standard of taste, and after a lengthy debate decided the answer is yes, given that we all share a special faculty: taste. Hume's preoccupation with aesthetics was linked to ethics, and in *A Treatise of Human Nature* he argued that moral and aesthetic evaluations are expressions of sentiment and not, as the rationalists would have it, intellectual intuition. Therefore deciding whether 'X' is good or bad or beautiful or ugly is an expression of approval or disapproval that has nothing to do with reality. Nevertheless, it is part of our human nature to seek pleasure and avoid pain, which occurs in accordance with forces within our nature, which can be regarded as a common denominator in all human beings, a good starting point.

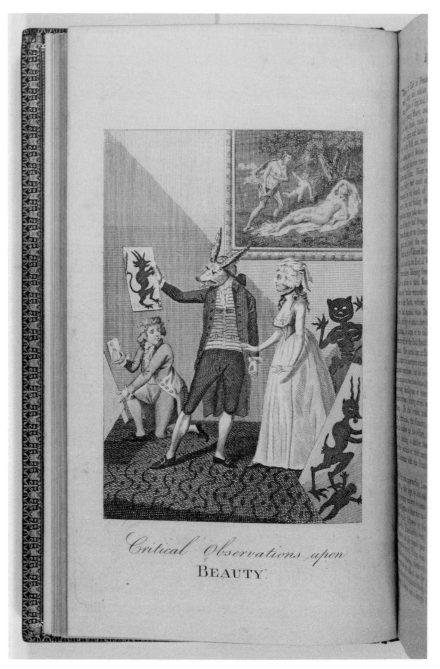

Figure 4 'Critical Observations upon Beauty', *Bon Ton Magazine: or Microscope of Fashion and Folly*, Volume V, March 1795, courtesy of the Lewis Walpole Library, Yale University.

In *Of the Standard of Taste*, Hume started by acknowledging that taste is a matter of opinion and therefore differs from person to person, but as seeking pleasure is also part of our nature then so is seeking 'standards of taste' in beauty. But what is beauty? Hume argued that beauty is 'no quality in things themselves, it exists merely in the mind which contemplates them; and each mind perceives a different beauty' (Hume, 1965, p. 6).

Therefore, what could be a better than expressing philosophically the famous adage that 'Beauty is in the eyes of the beholder'? But this cannot be the whole story and indeed it is not, for Hume argued that there is a 'certain common sense, which opposes it' and therefore nobody would 'assert an equality of genius and elegance between Ogilby and Milton, or Bunyan and Addison'. It is interesting to pause over this choice of examples, because while Milton may be a familiar name, Ogilby, Bunyan and even Addison are unknown to the twenty-first century reader. We can however appreciate Hume's point that such a statement would be tantamount to maintaining 'a mole-hill to be as high as Teneriffe, or a pond as extensive as the ocean' (Hume, 1965, p. 7)

As a good empiricist, Hume argued that such evaluative judgements cannot be 'fixed by reasonings *a priori* or can be esteemed abstract conclusions of the understanding' because 'their foundation is the same with that of all the practical sciences, experience' (Hume, 1965, p. 7). It follows that aesthetic judgements too are empirical and Hume neatly introduced here the concept of the 'qualified observer' – our modern critic – who alone can create order in the seeming chaos of the multitude of subjective responses to art, because, 'It appears, then, that amidst all the variety and caprice of taste, there are certain general principles of approbation or blame, whose influence a careful eye may trace in all operations of the mind' (Hume, 1965, p. 9).

Who are the critics?

Who then are the critics? Hume was very specific about what he expected of his critic apart from delicacy of taste: experience, practice, lack of prejudice and good sense, without which the critic cannot do his job, and then Hume wondered, rhetorically no doubt, as he had the answer: 'Where are such critics to be found? by what marks are they to be known? how to distinguish them from pretenders?' But as an empiricist he did not see a problem for one simple reason: we are dealing with 'questions of fact, not of sentiment . . . Whether any particular person be endowed with good sense and a delicate imagination, free from prejudice, may often be the subject of dispute, and be liable to great discussion and inquiry: but that such a character is valuable and estimable, will be agreed in by all mankind' (Hume, 1965, p. 18). Such men, although rare, are easily distinguished in society 'by the soundness of their understanding, and the superiority of their faculties above the rest of mankind' (Hume, 1965, p. 18). Finally, Hume allowed for two additional 'sources of variation' to be considered in the critic: 'different humours of particular men' and 'the particular manners and opinions of our age and country'. With regard to the former he gave a delightful example illustrating the impact of age on the critic's response to art:

> A young man, whose passions are warm, will be more sensibly touched with amorous and tender images, than a man more advanced in years, who takes pleasure in wise, philosophical reflections, concerning the conduct of life, and moderation of the passions. At twenty, Ovid may be the favourite author, Horace at forty, and perhaps Tacitus at fifty (Hume, 1965, p. 20).

But it is with regard to the second that Hume made a seminal observation, anticipating Hegel's historicism, whereby the critic belongs to his times and must therefore reflect manners, mores and everything pertaining to it. A profound yet simple point, and who put it more poignantly than Charles Baudelaire a century later, when he invited painters to depict the romantic men and women of their own times instead of the endless Greeks and Romans of *pompier* or *salon* art. The critic therefore must address these differences as rooted in the historical and cultural context that produced them and the example he chose was attire: 'Must we throw aside the pictures of our ancestors, because of their ruffs and farthingales' (Hume, 1965, p. 21).

In one respect, however, 'morality and decency' (and here the Scottish Calvinist moralist became dogmatic) such concessions cannot be applied and therefore even the grandest poets are not exempt: 'the want of humanity and of decency, so conspicuous in the characters drawn by several of the ancient poets, even sometimes by Homer and the Greek tragedians, diminishes considerably the merit of their noble performances, and gives modern authors an advantage over them' (Hume, 1965, p. 23).

Edmund Burke's *A Philosophical Enquiry* is justly regarded as 'the most famous investigation into the nature of the aesthetic qualities (Beardsley, 1966, p. 193). Written with youthful enthusiasm, the book became a popular and without doubt much debated subject around the dinner tables of 'gentle' society. In the 'Introduction on Taste', Burke provided a definition of taste whose aims were to establish inter-subjectively valid standards of taste (Beardsley, 1966, p. 193): 'But to cut off all pretence for cavilling, I mean by the word Taste no more than that faculty, or those faculties of the mind which are affected with, or which form a judgment of the works of imagination and the elegant arts' (Burke, 1990, p. 13).

Burke considered that taste, like reason is 'the same in all human creatures' and therefore a sort of 'logic of Taste' could be devised as the basis for criticism otherwise, as Clive Bell put it later, 'we gibber' (Bell, 2005). Burke said: 'If Taste has no fixed principles, if the imagination is not affected according to some invariable and certain laws, our labour is like to be employed to very little purpose; as it must be judged an useless, if not an absurd undertaking, to lay down rules for caprice, and to set up for a legislator of whims and fancies' (Burke, 1990, p. 12).

Given that men relate to external objects through 'the Senses, the Imagination; and the Judgment' (Burke, 1990, p. 12) Burke then expanded the definition of taste to incorporate them as well:

On the whole it appears to me that what is called Taste, in its most general acceptation, is not a simple idea, but is partly made up of a perception of the primary pleasures of sense, of the secondary pleasures of the imagination, and of the conclusions of the reasoning faculty, concerning the various relations of these and concerning the human passions, manners and actions (Burke, 1990, p. 22).

Part 1 of *A Philosophical Enquiry* was dedicated to the passions, which play a seminal part in Burke's account of taste; he distinguished two main categories, pain and pleasure, defined as 'simple ideas incapable of definition' (Burke, 1990, p. 30), which he regarded as the regulators of all emotions. But they are both positive, so one is not defined as a (lack) negation of the other. Thus the distinction between the two categories of the sublime and the beautiful – which were the subject of his enquiry – is that which we have between two types of agreeable sensation: 'positive pleasure' derived from experiencing the beautiful and another emotion Burke called 'delight', by which he meant the 'removal or diminution of pain', which is to be found at the heart of the experience of the sublime: 'As I make use of the word *Delight* to express the sensation which accompanies the removal of pain or danger so when I speak of positive pleasure, I shall for the most part call it simply *Pleasure*' (Burke, 1990, p. 34).

Apart from the passions in our breasts, Burke discussed those which belong to 'self-preservation' and society. As mentioned earlier, he made the distinction between *the society of sexes*, which answers the purposes of propagation, for example self-preservation, which turn on pain and danger, and *general society*, shared by men with other animals and the passions they engender, are simply to do with sex and gratification. These pleasures can be 'rapturous and violent . . . the highest pleasure of the senses', yet Burke added, perhaps with a smile, the absence of this particular kind of pleasure 'scarce amounts to uneasiness and except at particular times, I do not think it affects at all' (Burke, 1990, p. 37).

The passion at the heart of our experience of the sublime is terror, which always produces delight when it does not press too close to danger (an important point Burke returned to later), but this kind of delight is not exactly a pleasure because it turns on pain. Burke then produced a list of sensible qualities that make objects terrible, among them obscurity, power, privation, emptiness and greatness of dimension.

The passion at the heart of our experience of beauty is love, and Burke defined beauty as 'that quality or those qualities in bodies by which they cause love, or some passion similar to it' (Burke, 1990, p. 83). He proceeded with the same careful consideration to define what kinds of sensible qualities that make objects beautiful and started with a humorous refutation of the time honoured Greek definition of beauty as symmetry and proportion and the title of Section II (Part III) is 'Proportion not the cause of beauty in vegetables' (Burke, 1990, p. 84):

> What proportion do we discover between the stalks and the leaves of flowers, or between the leaves and the pistils? How does the slender stalk of the rose agree with the bulky head under which it bends? But the rose is a beautiful flower; and can we undertake to say that it does not owe a great deal of its beauty even to that disproportion? The rose is a large flower, yet it grows upon a small shrub; the flower of the apple is very small, and it grows upon a large tree; yet the rose and the apple blossom are both beautiful and the plants that bear them are most engagingly attired notwithstanding this disproportion (Burke, 1990, p. 86).

This quotation may very well be one of the sources of the many printed caricatures of assorted vegetables, fortifications and rose gardens on women's high wigs and 'head-dresses' as published in England and France in the late 1760s and 1770s.

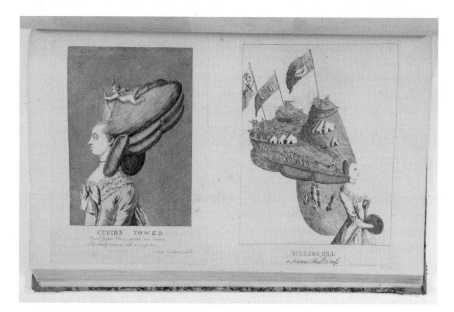

Figure 5 'Cupid's Tower', March 1776, and 'Bunker's Hill or America's Head Dress', *Darly's Comic Prints*, 1776, courtesy of the Lewis Walpole Library, Yale University.

As with proportion, Burke argued that fitness and perfection are not causes of beauty, but then he provided a list we find in Section XII (Part III) entitled 'The real cause of beauty', giving his answer: beautiful objects are small, with smoothness, gradual variation, delicacy and beauty in colour (Burke, 1990, pp. 102–7).

Having established what physical qualities produce the experience of the sublime and of beauty respectively, Burke provided in Part IV a psychological analysis of how the sublime and the beautiful are produced, which we find in Section I, entitled 'Of the efficient cause of the sublime and beautiful' (Burke, 1990, p. 117). While his terminology may sound arcane, he returned to the point made earlier, similar to Aristotle's argument that our pleasure in watching a tragedy is its remoteness from the reality of our lives. Pain can be a cause of delight:

> if the pain and terror are so modified as not to be actually noxious; if the pain is not carried to violence, and the terror is not conversant about the present destruction of the person, as these emotions clear the arts, whether fine, or gross, of a dangerous and troublesome incumbrance, they are capable of producing delight; not pleasure, but a sort of delightful horror, a sort of tranquillity tinged with terror, which as it belongs to self-preservation is one of the strongest of all passions. Its object is the sublime. Its highest degree I call *astonishment*; the subordinate degrees are *awe, reverence*, and *respect*, which by the very etymology of the words shew [sic] from what source they are derived, and how they stand distinguished from positive pleasure (Burke, 1990, p. 123).

In this masterful passage, Burke clinched the paradoxical nature of the experience of the sublime, as Aristotle had done before him and Kant after him.

Immanuel Kant: *Critique of Judgement* (1790)

Immanuel Kant (1724–1804) is considered to be the greatest of modern philosophers whose influence permeated every sphere of philosophy, not least philosophical aesthetics. He lived in Königsberg in Eastern Prussia all his life and he was a man of such regular habits that people used to set their watches by him as he went for his constitutional every day at the same time, with one exception: 'On one occasion his time-table was disrupted for several days; this was when he was reading *Emile*. He said that he had to read Rousseau's book several times, because, at first reading, the beauty of the style prevented him from noticing the matter' (Russell, 1979, p. 678).

Kant was profoundly influenced by the writings of Jean-Jacques Rousseau and by David Hume's empiricism. In a way, his trilogy of 'critical philosophy' is considered a revolution in which the centrality of metaphysics is established; here he replied to Hume's famous statement ('Hume's fork') from *An Enquiry Concerning Human Understanding*, that metaphysical propositions deserve more than being committed to the flames, because they contain a great deal more than 'sophistry and confusion'.

Kant presented a new classification, not of propositions but of what he called judgements (asserted propositions). Apart from the distinction also used by Hume between analytic (deductive) and synthetic (empirical) propositions, he introduced an additional distinction for judgements, between *a priori* (before experience) and *a posteriori* (after experience). Thus judgements can be analytic *a priori* (as they are also in Hume's account) or synthetic *a posteriori* (as they are also in Hume's account); postulating analytic *a posteriori* judgements is a logical contradiction, and so we are left with one other category: synthetic *a priori*, which are the judgements that deal not only with the three central issues of metaphysics, God, freedom and immortality, but other judgements, among them the ethical and aesthetic, to which he dedicated volumes 2 *Critique of Practical Reason* and 3 *Critique of Judgement* respectively.

Critique of Judgement dealt with the concepts of beauty and the sublime and in his very methodical way he divided the book into a first part, 'Critique of the Aesthetical Judgement', and a second part, 'Critique of the Teleological Judgement'.

Part 1 in turn has two parts: 'The analytic of the aesthetical judgement' and 'The dialectic of the aesthetical judgement', the latter containing an important section entitled 'Of beauty as the symbol of morality', in which Kant, like most of his predecessors, going back to Plato, presented the beautiful as symbol of the good, and ultimately God.

Kant asked the very question central to philosophical aesthetics that bothered all philosophers, starting with Alexander Baumgarten: how are aesthetic judgements possible at all, given that they are subjective (as Hume beautifully put it) but claim universal validity (aspire to be inter-subjectively valid)? His answer was facilitated by the new synthetic *a priori* type of judgement that he devised to deal with metaphysical issues. Kant's definition of beauty was as a perceptual form whose subjective finality renders it disinterested (in quality), universal (in quantity), categorical (in relation) and necessary (in modality).

Thus regarding quality, most aesthetic judgements reference personal avowals of pleasure and pain and only some aesthetic judgements are judgements of our special faculty 'taste', defined as 'the faculty of judging an object or a method of representing it by an entirely disinterested satisfaction or dissatisfaction. The object of such satisfaction is called beautiful' (Kant, 1966, p. 45). The concept of disinterestedness itself has quite a long pedigree, as we find it already postulated by the Third Earl of Shaftesbury and the empiricists whence Kant borrowed it.

The aesthetic judgement relating to quantity is universal and this is important because it replies to the key question of rendering to a subjective response an inter-subjective validity. Kant argued that when we speak of 'X' being beautiful, we use the word as if it were a property in the object, which it is not; instead my statement reports my personal aesthetic satisfaction. But this is a special aesthetic satisfaction that is disinterested and so equal in all, justifying my statement: 'this is beautiful' instead of 'this gives me disinterested satisfaction'. The transcendental question here is: how can such a judgement be possible? How can a statement like 'this is beautiful', in fact reporting my personal aesthetic satisfaction, be universal, in the same way as a logical judgement such as 'This flower is a rose'? Kant makes the point that 'the solution of this question is the key to the critique of taste, and so is worthy of all attention (Kant, 1966, p. 51). Here we refer to Kant's definition of cognitive faculties as developed in *The Critique of Pure Reason*, perfectly explained here:

> All rational beings are capable of cognition, which requires the connectibility of two faculties, imagination (to gather together the manifold of sense-intuition) and understanding (to unify these representations by means of concepts) . . . There arises a state of mind in which there is a feeling of the free play of the representative powers in a given representation with reference to a cognition in general (Beardsley, 1966, pp. 214–15).

Regarding relation, beauty can be regarded as without a category (concept-less), a kind of purposiveness without purpose (perceived without a purpose). Thus the same purposive whole can be subject to a teleological judgement and a judgement of aesthetic taste. Observing a graceful galloping horse we may observe its perfection as utility of best function (its graceful long legs perfect for racing) or we may just say 'what a beautiful thing', not worrying what it is. In other words, the mind does not engage with classification, but allows for harmonious interplay of what the eyes see. Finally, the concept of modality is necessary: beauty is that which without a concept is recognized as the object of necessary pleasure. Thus the synthetic *a priori* concept of taste is justified as follows: the experience of beauty is *necessary* and *universal* which makes it *a priori* and also disinterested, and concept-less (purposiveness without purpose), which makes it *analytical.*

As Miller argued elsewhere (Miller, 2007, pp. 38–9), if we employ one of the three partial definitions of beauty, that of relation, and use the famous concept of 'purposiveness without purpose', it will enable us to regard an object from the point of view of its final purpose (this chair is for sitting on) but we can also regard it as if it were devoid of purpose and enjoy it as something lovely to behold. Paul Poiret's beautiful dresses *qua* dresses, to be worn by his clients, or Paul Poiret's beautiful dresses considered as objects of contemplation – in a way analogous to Kant's example of a beautiful horse *qua* horse, for example best fulfilling its function as racing horse or just something that pleases the eyes which happens to be a horse – can be placed under that concept, but need not be!

So with Kant's help, we conclude that clothes could after all be regarded at least in some cases as objects of aesthetic contemplation and could be (and at present often are) placed in a museum as objects of admiration, and of course they could be regarded as something that is highly desirable to be worn by fashionable women.

If dresses can be subjected to the judgement of taste, can we not provide them also with a critical vocabulary? This is exactly what happened during the nineteenth century, when Charles Baudelaire predicated 'charm' (used, we could argue, for the first time) as an evaluative expression, for example analogous to a term such as 'beautiful', and thus a critical vocabulary of fashion emerged for the first time, as will be argued in the following chapter.

5

CHARLES BAUDELAIRE: THE BEGINNING OF FASHION CRITICISM; THE ART CRITIC OF THE SALONS

Charles Baudelaire: the painter of modern life

Charles Baudelaire was the originator of the concept of *modernité*. In his essay 'Le Peintre de la vie moderne' (The Painter of Modern Life) dated between 1859 and 1860, and dedicated to the graphic artist and illustrator Constantin Guys, he provided 'one of the first and most profound analyses of *modernité*' (Lehmann, 2000, p. 5). This particular *salon* review became famous not so much for Baudelaire's critical analysis of Constantin Guys, the artist he singled out to have captured *modernité* in his *oeuvre*, but for two of the most often quoted definitions, those of 'beauty' and 'modernity': 'Beauty is made up, on the one hand, of an element that is eternal and invariable, though to determine how much there is it is extremely difficult, and, on the other, of a relative circumstantial element, which we may like to call, successively or at one and the same time, contemporaneity, fashion, morality, passion' (Baudelaire, 1972, p. 392).

From the definition of beauty, Baudelaire derived that of modernity: 'Modernity is the transient, the fleeting, the contingent: it is one half of art, the other being the eternal and the immovable' (Baudelaire, 1972, p. 403).

What has hitherto been overlooked is Baudelaire's comment, regarding not only sartorial fashion, but hairstyle, gesture, smile (histories of dress have been published, but we are yet to produce comprehensive histories of hairstyles, gestures or smiles!), and for that reason it deserves to be quoted in full. Baudelaire considered dress as the result of the historical and cultural matrix that produced it, in turn becoming its most faithful mirror. Dress, therefore, is informed by the contingent, pertaining to spatio-temporal modernity, rather than universal beauty:

> There was a form of modernity for every painter of the past; the majority of the fine portraits that remain to us from former times are clothed in the dress of their own day. They are perfectly harmonious works because the dress, the hairstyle, and even the gesture, the expression and the smile (each age has its carriage, its expression and its smile) form a whole, full of vitality. You have no right to despise this transitory fleeting element, the metamorphoses of which are so frequent, nor to dispense with it. (Baudelaire, 1972, p. 403).

Baudelaire wanted to break free from the constraints of the rules of the Academy established from its point of inception in 1648; more importantly, he wanted to shift the focus from the heroic and noble deeds which Academic painters were supposed to represent in order to inspire lofty thoughts in their viewers, via the Greeks, Romans and the mythological and biblical heroes of *illo termpore*, and represent people instead in their everyday costumes going about their everyday business. Related to sartorial fashion, Baudelaire introduced for the first time the topic of cosmetics, arguing against Jean-Jacques Rousseau's idealistic view that nature is superior to the corrupting influence of culture, nowhere put more beautifully than in the opening lines of *The Social Contract*, first published in 1762: 'Man is born free, and everywhere he is in chains. One man thinks himself the master of others, but remains more of a slave than they are' (Rousseau quoted by Russell, 1979, p. 669). Rousseau's argument for a society based on democratic principles as a lesser evil regarding man's individual freedom can be traced back to the beginnings of his literary career in 1750 when he won a prize for an essay in which he argued that 'science, letters and the arts are the worst enemies of morals, and, by creating wants, are the sources of slavery; for how can chains be imposed on those who go naked, like American savages?' (Russell, 1979, p. 662). Voltaire, to whom Rousseau sent his essay, did not quite subscribe to Rousseau's notion that the state of nature can be a desirable alternative to culture and promptly replied: 'Never was such cleverness used in the design of making us all stupid. One longs, in reading your book, to walk on all fours. But as I have lost that habit for more than sixty years, I feel unhappily the impossibility of resuming it' (Voltaire in Russell, 1979, p. 663).

Baudelaire, like Voltaire before him, preferred 'culture' to 'nature', and regarded fashion and cosmetics as its elevated expression, and therefore the perfect embodiment of the two strands which defined *modernité*, the transitory and the eternal; through fashion Baudelaire discovered 'the elemental dialectics that determine modernity: the coexistence of the ephemeral and the sublime, the fugitive and the profound' (Lehmann, 2000, p. 8). In 'The Painter of Modern Life', Baudelaire revealed also that he researched historic fashion plates in order to uncover the same elements of the eternal and the transitory that informed fashion:

> I have here in front of me a series of fashion plates, the earliest dating from the Revolution, the most recent from the Consulate or thereabouts. These costumes, which many thoughtless people, the sort of people who are grave without true gravity, find highly amusing, have a double kind of charm, artistic and historical . . . Man comes in the end to look like his ideal image of himself. These engravings can be translated into beauty or ugliness: in ugliness they become caricatures; in beauty, antique statues.
>
> (Baudelaire, 1972, p. 391).

It appears that the fashion plates referenced by Baudelaire were produced by Pierre de La Mésangère when he was editor of the early nineteenth-century *Journal des Dames et des Modes*, and Baudelaire 'confesses in a letter that he used the magazine 'not just for the images, but for the text' (Lehmann, 2000, pp. 8–9). De La Mésangère was an artist, decorator and publisher of *Meubles et Objets de Goût*, a periodical published during the *Consulat, Directoire* and Napoléon I era. In this way Baudelaire revealed himself as one of the pioneers of the study of fashion ephemera and of the nineteenth-century draughtsmen and cartoonists who made fashion one of their central subjects.

Le Journal des Dames et des Modes was a particularly important publication because it captures a brief moment in the turbulent history of the French Revolution. It was founded in 1797 by Jean-Baptiste Selléque and then taken over by Pierre-Antoine Leboux de la Mésangère, former professor of the distinguished Collège Henri IV de La Flèche, who transformed it into an arbiter of taste and fashion at the Napoleonic court. The periodical, like so many others of its time, dwelt not just on dress fashions but covered fashions in all things including the newly complex 'neo-classical' curtain treatments and bed-hangings so beloved of the post-Revolutionary period. Arlette Farge, in her research on public opinion and the press in the French Revolutionary period, called this new and greatly expanded zone of print the 'informational sphere' (Farge, 1994, p. 198). Although Farge was referring mainly to Revolutionary mantra, the right to judge taste in sartorial fashions was also now on the agenda, perhaps for the first time. Baudelaire's confession in the mid-nineteenth century that he was as interested in images as he was in the text, points to the fact that he wanted to understand fashion not only from a visual and aesthetic point of view, but also in its historical context: 'Baudelaire starts by establishing fashion as an art form in itself and as a timely reminder of the past, a past that is far from gone: it lives on through the clothes and is revived in the details of sartorial styles created anew each season' (Lehmann, 2000, p. 9).

The fashion plate had indeed gathered momentum during the eighteenth century. In 1779 a collection of fashion plates published between 1778 and

1787, by Jacques Esnauts and Michel Rapilly as separate albums containing six fashion plates each, were published in a book reproducing 96 prints from the previous sixteen albums. Its lengthy title was *Gallerie des modes et des costumes français dessinés d'après nature, Gravés par le plus Célèbres Artistes en ce genre, et colorés avec le plus grand soin par Madame Le Beau. Ouvrage commence en l'année 1778. A Paris, chez le Srs Esnauts et Rapilly, rue St. Jacques, à la Ville de coutances. Avec priv. Du Roi* (Morini, 2006, p. 29). The specific point made in the title that these outfits were designed 'after nature' testifies to the fact that they were representing what was actually worn in the streets of Paris. In order to emphasize this new approach to fashion illustration, the outfits worn by the fashion-conscious Parisians were represented in charming *tableaux vivants*, as if 'frozen in a moment in their lives' (Morini, 2006, p. 30). Moreover, the images were created by prominent visual artists, among them Claude-Louis Desrais, Pierre Thomas Leclerc, François-Louis-Joseph Watteau (grandnephew of Antoine Watteau) and Augustin de Saint-Aubin (Morini, 2006, p. 32); this suggests the strong influence of figurative painting in their creation.

This idea has been famously developed by the literature expert Anne Hollander in her renowned book *Seeing Through Clothes*, in which she resolutely states that fashion is a form of art: 'Dress is a form of visual art, a creation of images with the visible self as its medium' and consequently 'the art of dress has its own autonomous history, a self-perpetuating flow of images derived from other images. But any living image of a clothed body derives essentially from a picture' (Hollander, 1993, p. 311). As the backdrop of Hollander's innovative claim lies the philosopher Heinrich Wölfflin, pupil of the father of modern art history, Jacob Burckhardt, who wrote that the shift from a 'natural loveliness' to the 'graver antique beauty' of the sixteenth century (Burckhardt in Cropper, 1998, p. 2) was about people changing in and of themselves: 'that man himself has changed even in his outward, bodily form; and the real kernel of a style is in the new outlook upon the human body and in new ideas about deportment and movement' (Wölfflin in Cropper, 1998, p. 2).

If we pursue this reasoning to its logical conclusion, the beautiful outfits represented in these fashion plates 'drawn after nature' in Esnauts and Rapilly's albums provided just such templates for people to imitate, and that included not only the clothes but the postures and the movements; in other words, the entire 'look'. Before the advent of photography, the moving images and even the printing press, 'elegant people wished to live up to the exquisitely conceived and executed versions of themselves painted by Van Eyck, Van Dyck, Ingres, Nicolas Hilliard, or John Singer Sargent' (Hollander, 1993, p. 315).

Artists' sketches are singled out by Hollander as a visual source for capturing the mores and manners of the period: 'they are references to figures, notes for poses and groupings, generalizations out of the mind's eye' and the artist singled out as excelling in the mastery of capturing the fleetingness of a moment is

Figure 6 Watteau fils [François Louis Joseph] (French, Valenciennes), designer; Nicolas Dupin, engraver: 'La belle engagée par les discours touchans [sic] les tendres sollicitations d'un aimable Séducteur . . . chapeau a la Henri IV et vetue d'une robe a la Marguerite', *46e cahier* [46th series] *de Gallerie des Modes et Costumes Français; Costumes Francois, 41e suite d'Habillements a la mode en 1785* [41st suite of fashionable dress of 1785], Esnauts et Rapilly, France, hand-coloured engraving on laid paper, 27.6 × 21.6 cm (10 7/8 × 8 1/2in.), © Museum of Fine Arts, Boston, The Elizabeth Day McCormick Collection 44.1623.

Figure 7 Pierre-Thomas LeClerc, *dessinateur*, [draughtsman, French c.1740, after 1799] and Charles Emmanuel Jean Baptiste Patas, *graveur*, [engraver, 1744–1802], 'Vêtement dit à la créole' ['clothing said to be in the Creole manner'], *Gallerie des Modes et Costumes français dessinés d'après nature, gravés par les plus celebres artistes en ce genre, et colorés avec le plus grand soin par Madame Le Beau, planche* (plate) no. 161 in the 27th series (*cahier*) 'de costumes français – 21e suite d'habillemens [sic] à la mode en 1779', 1779, 38.7 × 25.1 cm (15 1/4 × 9 7/8 in.), © Museum of Fine Arts Boston, The Elizabeth Day McCormick Collection 44.1438.

Constantin Guys, 'exalted by Baudelaire' (Hollander, 1993, p. 317). However, Baudelaire's choice of Constantin Guys' art as the exemplary signifier of *modernité* has been challenged by none other than Edouard Manet, who justifiably regarded himself as the painter of modernity because he was the creator of the prototype of the *Parisienne* as its embodiment.

In opposition to the hypothesis that during the nineteenth century the fine arts were the inspiration for fashion, we witness a reverse process, whereby fashion plates themselves became a source of research for artists. Marie Simon makes the case that it was an interest in delineating contemporary fashion that unified the very complex picture of nineteenth-century French painting, from the official or *pompier* art of Carolus-Duran and Gervex, to the *avant-garde* practice of Impressionism and Post-Impressionism. She also argues that the dissemination of the fashion plate encouraged the development of a new freedom in the construction of the portrait genre. The paintings of the Impressionist artist Eugène Boudin, for example, resemble the settings of fashion plates, as well as recalling the fashion journalism of Stéphane Mallarmé in *La Dernière Mode* (1874). The 'realist' novelist Emile Zola attacked the less painterly and rather mechanical style of Alfred Stevens as being nothing more than a cheap fashion plate on display in a *salon*. Lehmann notes the incredible example of Caillebotte, whose sketch *Study of a Couple under an Umbrella* (1877) (private collection) blocks out the male dress, but leaves the definition of the female clothes blank, in order to leave them to the last minute ready for incorporation into the final picture *Rue de Paris* (Lehmann, 2000, p. 82). Critics such as William Bürger (Théophile Thoré) reflected on the paintings of Whistler as motives for the influence of lived fashion.

An example recently exhibited proves the point: two plates reproduced in *La mode illustrée*, dated 31 July 1870 and 7 May 1871 respectively, both in private collections, represent two afternoon outfits and two promenade outfits put to good use in two paintings by Paul Cézanne (exhibition *L'Impressionisme et la mode*, Paris 2013, p. 122), the first entitled *La Conversation ou les deux soeurs* (1870–71) and the second entitled *La Promenade* (1871). In both instances the painter copied the images from the fashion magazine very accurately, although in the first instance he added two young men seen from the back in the background, dressed in dandyish attire. The outfits of the two young sisters, one seated, the other standing in a graceful pose, are copied with great accuracy from the fashion plates, including colour, details of the flounces of the bustles and their posture, and the same holds true of the second example. Even the backgrounds, including trees and plants, have been copied by Cézanne into his paintings, almost without change. It has to be said, however, that he abstracted the women's faces in such a way that they cannot be considered saccharine. We are in the fortunate situation of being able to compare two sets of images, the first from a fashion magazine, the second the work of one of the greatest modernist painters – during the early stages of his career when he was still grappling to find ways to implement his complicated theories in his paintings.

What emerges is that it was the artist in search of *modernité* who took his cue from the fashion plate and not the other way round. That was the reason – according to one argument – for the emergence during the 1860s of the prototype of a very special woman: *la Parisienne*. Moulded by Gustave Courbet and Edouard Manet's paintings as well as the vast amounts of literary and critical writings produced on and about her, she became 'a fashion diktat', whose fashions more than her face commanded attention (Tinterow in Groom, 2013, p. 32). Indeed, Cézanne's attempt to frame *la Parisienne* in his youthful paintings by taking his cue from fashion magazines in order to find the signifiers to represent her was inspired also by Edouard Manet's celebrated *La Musique aux Tuileries* painted in 1862, which became not only the true manifesto of Baudelaire's concept of *modernité*, but more importantly constituted 'an effort to draw up the catalogue of Parisian types' (Tinterow in Groom, 2013, p. 31). Its theme was the Parisian *bougeoisie* at work and play and they provided the inspiration and even the template to his Impressionist contemporaries: 'Monet, Renoir, Paul Cézanne and Degas' (Tinterow in Groom, 2013, p. 31).

But the Impressionists were inspired also by the writings of Charles Baudelaire and his bold 'diktat' (for this is what it had become) with regard to modern life, that 'the representation of contemporary *mores* and costumes were equivalent to *modernité*' (Tinterow in Groom, 2013, p. 31). What disappointed Manet was that Baudelaire failed to see that it was his work rather than that of 'the improbable Constantin Guys' who succeeded as the '*peintre de la vie moderne*' (painter of modern life). Baudelaire ignored the general consensus of fellow critics and 'was blinded to the limitations of Guys who was at best a facile draftsman and watercolorist and a clever improvisator because Guys combined contemporaneity with grace and charm. Nor was Baudelaire able to comprehend the art of his friend Edouard Manet' (Holt, 1966, p. 172). Another reason for his short-sightedness may have been justified by the fact that 'Baudelaire was too much the product of the period of Louis-Philippe to be able to comprehend the path travelled by Manet; his illness in 1865, followed by his premature death two years later, prevented him from acquiring the necessary perspective' (Tinterow in Groom, 2013, p. 31).

The emergence of a critical vocabulary of fashion writing: *charm*

Charles Baudelaire used the concept of 'charm' by predicating it of sartorial dress dating from the revolutionary period, which, he argued, 'have a double kind of charm, artistic and historical' (Baudelaire, 1972, p. 391), returning to it again in a more specific manner, and predicating it of fashion: 'All fashions are charming'. He proceeds to say that if this offends by being too absolute, one can replace it with 'legitimately charming in their day' (Baudelaire, 1972, pp. 426–7). In order to solve what appears as a paradoxical statement, Baudelaire argued that if a universal statement such as 'All X are Y' might give offence because of its apodictic character and would not be appropriate to the time-based nature of fashion, he would replace it with the relative clause, thus historicizing the universal claim 'all fashions are charming' to 'legitimately charming in their day'. The shift from timeless universal (all) to historically particular (in their day) enabled Baudelaire to conflate further his definition of fashion with those of beauty and modernity respectively – whose dual nature incorporating both a universal and an historical dimension summed up in the case of beauty as 'contemporaneity, fashion, morality, passion'.

Charm me

The dictionary definition of 'charm' is the quality of pleasing, of fascinating or attracting people'. Charm is also the quality to attract or fascinate; delight greatly; finally charm is also about enchantment (*Collins English Dictionary*, 2005, p. 287). The question is whether Baudelaire used 'charm' as an aesthetic quality (analogous to beauty), and a case could be made in the affirmative, because he may have used 'charm' analogous to 'beauty', as not pertaining to the object, but as constituting a subjective response, for example a personal avowal of pleasure. If we accept Immanuel Kant's distinction that only some aesthetic judgements – those that express disinterested pleasure – are judgements of taste, then, as Baudelaire argued, each fashion (from their specific historical period) can be regarded as 'a new striving, more or less well conceived, after beauty, an approximate statement of an ideal' (Baudelaire, 1972, p. 426). Can we not consider, then, that charm, when predicated of fashion, is an aesthetic quality, albeit with different connotations from beauty, one of which was introduced by Baudelaire himself:

> But, if we want to enjoy fashions thoroughly, we must not look upon them as dead things; we might as well admire a lot of old clothes hung, up, limp and inert, like the skin of St. Bartholomew, in the cupboard of a second-hand-clothes dealer. They must be pictured as full of the life and vitality of the beautiful women that wore them. Only in that way can we give them meaning and value (Baudelaire, 1972, p. 426).

Baudelaire then argues for the necessity of a functional dimension for dress which only makes visual sense when worn by the beautiful women they were meant for. But he is considerably more subtle, because when he was reflecting on the old fashion plates dating from the Revolution, the key point was that the aesthetic pleasure he derived from them had a 'double kind of charm artistic and historical' – their beauty was not only visual, resulting from ruffles or the detailing of a coat, but also dependent on the whole attire, the gestures, the features of the face; reflecting the 'moral attitude' as well as' the aesthetic value of the time', a totality that is expressive of its *Zeitgeist*.

But where did Baudelaire find the concept of charm and why did he decide to use it in connection with fashion? The answer is that he purloined it from his own poetry, for the simple reason that no specialized vocabulary for fashion existed at the time. And so Baudelaire had to invent his own, and indeed he did; we find 'charm' used with much enthusiasm in that infamous piece of poetry *Les fleurs du mal*. We selected two poems by way of example (Baudelaire, 1998, p. 123). This is 'Song of the Afternoon':

> A censer's faint perfume
> Prowls along your skin;
> You charm as evening charms,
> Warm and shadowy Nymph
>
> Under your satin shoes
> Your charming silken feet,
> I place myself, my joy,
> My genius and my fate

Baudelaire was prosecuted for this poem, and he sought redress by writing directly to the Empress Eugénie, who assisted in having the fine reduced and raised money for the poet (McQueen). The great figure of Second Empire high fashion, Eugénie, might have met the poet at the literary *salon* of Princesse Julie Bonaparte, or at least have been familiar with his work as she was extremely culturally attuned (Alison McQueen, private correspondence with Peter McNeil). The case indicates the complex circuits of cultural knowledge in that *mondaine* society, Paris.

The second example comes from a group of poems published in 1866 as *Les Épaves de Charles Baudelaire* ('Charles Baudelaire's Waifs' or 'Cast-offs') (Culler in Baudelaire, 1993, p. 46) entitled 'Lola de Valence', an homage to Edouard Manet's portrait of the Spanish dancer Lola de Valence, whose real name was Lola Melea, painted in 1862, and therefore topical (Baudelaire, 1993, p. 311):

> One sees such beauties everywhere one goes
> I know, my friends, desire hesitates;
> But in Lola de Valence radiates
> The rare charm of a jewel of black and rose.

Charles Baudelaire, critic of the salons

Baudelaire belongs to the Romantic movement, which emerged in nineteenth-century Europe, as a reaction against neo-classicism and the primacy of reason dominated by order, harmony and the intellect. They were replaced with the primacy of emotion, dominated by passions, exoticism and a return to 'Gothic' as a source of inspiration for literature and the visual arts. In Section II of the extensive review of the 1846 *Salon* entitled 'What is Romanticism?', Baudelaire had this to say on the matter: 'Properly speaking Romanticism lies neither in the subject an artist chooses nor in his exact copying of truth, but in the way he feels. Where artists were outward-looking, they should have looked inward, as the only way to find it. For me, Romanticism is the most recent, the most up-to-date expression of beauty' (Baudelaire, 1972, p. 52).

If Romanticism did indeed find its best expression in the sketch – as 'the least premeditated form of art – and thus to the free handling of materials which revealed in the most direct manner possible the individuality of the artist's 'touch' (Honour and Fleming, 1982, p. 482), that might explain the real reason why Baudelaire prioritized Constantin Guys above Edouard Manet. Baudelaire commented in fact that the former was a modest man who loved mixing with the crowds and being *incognito*; in other words he was the perfect Baudelarian *flâneur*, who did not even like to sign his works; instead – 'all his works are signed with his dazzling soul' (Baudelaire, 1972, p. 395).

Charles Baudelaire's career as a critic began with the 1845 *Salon* introduced with a sarcastic diatribe, not against the ignorant *bourgeoisie*, but against his fellow critics:

And to begin with, on the subject of that impertinent designation 'the bourgeois', we hereby let it be known that we do not at all subscribe to the prejudices of our important colleagues, with art at their finger-tips, who for several years now have been doing all they can to hurl anathemas at the inoffensive being, who would ask for nothing better than to appreciate good painting, if the gentlemen in question knew the art of making him understand it and if the artists showed him good painting more often (Baudelaire, 1972, p. 34).

It constituted also the perfect *apologia* for a newly appointed critic whose proper job is to make the poor 'inoffensive' *bourgeoisie* understand painting and who would be better at this job than he, Charles Baudelaire.

In the introductory section of this review, Baudelaire outlined also his methodology, whereby he would divide the paintings according to subject matter and arrange the artists 'according to the order and rating assigned them by public favour'. His starting point would be the best of them all, Eugène Delacroix, and his historical paintings: 'M. Delacroix is decidedly the most original painter of both ancient and modern times' (Baudelaire, 1972, p. 35). He brings colour into focus by referring to an article written by his friend Théophile Gautier about the painter Thomas Couture, in which he distinguished two types of drawing: 'the drawing of the colourists and the drawing of the draughtsmen' – whose techniques are opposite, although 'it is quite possible to draw with high-key colour, just as one may be able to build up harmonious masses of colour, and yet remain essentially a draughtsman'. Baudelaire chose Peter Paul Rubens, the great colourist, as his example, because he 'renders effectively, renders perfectly, the movement, physiognomy, the illusive and delicate character of nature, all things that the draughtsmanship of Raphael never renders'. Delacroix, like Rubens, was an excellent draughtsman and Baudelaire considered that only two other men in Paris 'draw as well as M. Delacroix – the one in an analogous manner, the other adopting a contrary method. The one is M. Daumier, the caricaturist; the other M. Ingres, the great painter, the cunning admirer of Raphael' (Baudelaire, 1972, pp. 37–8). Daumier is very pertinent within our study as he is perhaps the greatest artistic chronicler of the anti-intellectual 'man in the street' who 'knows it all' – the *bourgeois* philistine.

What is the good of criticism?

Baudelaire started his review of *Salon of 1846* with a witty oration in praise of the very bourgeois to whom he dedicated his *salon* review, because 'any book that does not appeal to the majority, in numbers and intelligence, is a stupid book' (Baudelaire, 1972, p. 49). He introduced two additional new sections, one entitled 'What is the good of criticism?' and the other 'On colour'. In the former Baudelaire re-introduced the debates about the importance of the public role of art that emerged during the Enlightenment with the revival in 1737 of the *salons*, which were instrumental in producing alongside the established disciplines of aesthetics and art history the new discipline of art criticism (Harrison, Wood and Gaiger, 2000, p. 425). Baudelaire accused the artists of bearing grudges against critics they regarded as unable either to teach the stupid bourgeoisie an art they were not interested in, or indeed to be able to explain it to them; and yet, Baudelaire added at the end, it is the critics who 'created' so many artistic reputations:

> The artist's first grudge against criticism is that it can teach nothing to the bourgeois who wants neither to paint nor to versify, nor has it anything to teach art, whose offspring it is. And yet how many artists of today owe to it alone their poor little reputations! That perhaps is the chief reproach to be made to it (Baudelaire, 1972, pp. 49–50).

AU MUSÉE DU LOUVRE, — par H. Daumier.

UN AMATEUR DU DIMANCHE.

— Ah! si j'avais tous ces vieux tableaux, comme je vendrais tous ces beaux cadres'...

Figure 8 Honoré Daumier, *Un Amateur du Dimanche* (A Sunday Amateur) 'At the Museum of the Louvre': 'Oh! if I had all these old pictures, how I could sell all these beautiful frames!', 1865, lithograph (gillotype), 21.6 × 17.2 cm, National Gallery of Victoria, Melbourne, Felton Bequest, 1930.

Baudelaire then presented his own notion of what the critic should do by employing a process of elimination to start with; ideal criticism should be 'entertaining and poetic', but that would be inappropriate for the arts and better employed 'for books of poetry and for readers of poetry'. Nevertheless, 'criticism proper' must also be 'engaged' in the sense of 'partial, passionate, political, that is to say it must adopt an exclusive point of view, provided always the one adopted opens up the widest horizons' (Baudelaire, 1972, pp. 49–50).

The last paragraph of this section (Baudelaire, 1972, pp. 49–50) betrays Hegel's influence with regard to the importance of analysing art within its own historical matrix as well as the employment of the ascending spiral of his dialectical method, according to which the most recent historical period necessarily contains the highest expression of beauty hitherto achieved. Consequently, the best artists of the Romantic period to Hegel and Baudelaire would be those who incorporated in their art 'the greatest degree of romanticism possible'.

Understanding Hegel

Georg Wilhelm Friedrich Hegel (1770–1831) delivered lectures on aesthetics and history of art between 1818 and 1829 at the universities of Heidelberg and Berlin respectively, and published posthumously in 1835 under the title *Lectures on Aesthetics*.

Hegel defined beauty as the visual representation of the divine and therefore considered beautiful art to offer a perception of 'the divine' or 'what is godlike'. Simply and broadly stated, beauty is 'God's appearance' (Wicks in Beiser, 1995, p. 349). Hegel then provided a twofold classification of the arts, divided according to style into symbolic, classical, Romantic; and according to subject, into architecture, sculpture, painting, music and poetry, and then proceeded to construct permutations: thus architecture is considered as essentially 'symbolic', sculpture as 'classical', and the remainder as 'Romantic'. Hegel introduced two radical methods in his argument:

- historicism first applied to philosophy, whereby Hegel proposed a 'history' of philosophy, and thus by transforming 'history' into a category of thought, Hegel can be regarded as the inventor of the modern concept of histories of everything, and that includes art, whereby art, too, becomes subject to and determined by its historical matrix

- dialectical development, according to which each historical period necessarily surpasses the previous one in its upward striving to reach the absolute, which is of course the godhead.

According to this model, Romantic art, which comes after the symbolic and the classical, is superior to both of them, and therefore painting, which is the first visual art to be Romantic, is superior to architecture and sculpture. For Hegel, painting, music and poetry, as Romantic arts, can be regarded as the highest form of artistic expression. This leaves things such as fashion and the other applied arts somewhat out in the cold.

We find the Hegelian concept of dialectical development (or something very similar) used by Baudelaire, in the section 'What is the Good of Criticism?', by way of a reply:

Since every century, every people has achieved the expression of its own beauty and system of moral values, and if the word romanticism may be defined as the most up to date and the most modern expression of beauty, then, in the eyes of the reasonable and passionate critic, the great artist will be he who combines with the condition laid down above – namely naiveté, the greatest degree of romanticism possible (Baudelaire, 1972, p. 52).

The section following 'What is the Good of Criticism?' is entitled 'What is Romanticism?' – and here Baudelaire reiterated the point that Romanticism 'is the most recent, the most up-to-date expression of beauty', whose special characteristics reside in feeling, perfectly embodied in the work of Delacroix. But before Baudelaire turned his attention to Delacroix's paintings, he introduced another topic closely related to his Romanticism: 'colour'. In it, Baudelaire offered a foretaste of Symbolist theory, by providing a correspondence between colour and music:

Harmony is the basis of the theory of colour. Melody means unity of colour, in other words, of a colour scheme. A melody needs to be resolved, in other words, it needs a conclusion, which all the individual effects combine to produce. By this means a melody leaves an unforgettable memory in the mind. Most of our young colourists lack melody (Baudelaire, 1972, p. 57).

He perfected the theme of 'correspondence' between the senses later in his famed poem 'Correspondances', in *Fleurs du mal* – which became adopted as the manifesto of the Symbolist movement:

As the long echoes, shadowy, profound,
Heard from afar, blend in a unity,
Vast as the night, as sunlight's clarity,
So perfumes, colours, sounds may correspond.
Odours there are, fresh as a baby's skin,
Mellow as oboes, green as meadow grass,
Others corrupted, rich triumphant, full,
Having dimensions infinitely vast,
Frankincense, musk ambergris, Benjamin,
Singing the senses' rapture, and the soul's (Baudelaire, 1998, p. 19).

Charles Baudelaire was also one of the three writers, alongside Théophile Gautier and Gustave Flaubert, of an important movement that emerged at that time, first in France. It came to be known by the popular phrase *l'art pour l'art* (art for art's sake), and his volume of poetry *Les fleurs du mal*, first published in 1857, regarded as 'the bible of decadence', became also a manifesto of the movement that prioritized art and aesthetics above all else, as will be discussed in Chapter 6.

6

OSCAR WILDE AND THE APOSTLES OF AESTHETICISM

The sole object of art is the beautiful. Art abandons itself as soon as it shuns this.

Victor Cousin

When James Abbott McNeill Whistler was granted an exhibition at the Grosvenor Gallery in London in 1877, John Ruskin wrote the famous line in his publication *Fors Clavigera* (The Club-bearer): 'I have never seen and heard much of cockney impudence before now but never expected to hear a coxcomb ask two hundred guineas for flinging a pot of paint in the public's face.' Ruskin lost the case for libel but Whistler was awarded only one pound damages. Subsequently, he published *The Gentle Art of Making Enemies* (1890). This artistic episode marks the emergence of so called 'aesthetic formalism', which goes on to create new possibilities for making art but also for designing, wearing and writing about fashion. The first and great couturier Charles Frederick Worth, for example, made the claim that a *toilette* was akin to the creation of a painting. If that is the case, then a garment might have the possibility of being read within 'formal' terms derived from the language of the art world.

Philosophical aesthetics was generally perceived to have emerged with the German philosophers of the Enlightenment (although the British empiricists made their own substantial contribution to it) and therefore in a way became German 'cultural property', but that was to change with the doctrine of *l'art pour l'art* (art for art's sake), which emerged in French Romantic literature. Subsequently it spread via the writing of Charles Baudelaire – whose volume of poetry *Les fleurs de mal*, first published in 1857, so shocked the bourgeoisie that it came to be regarded as the bible of decadence. The leading figures who rendered it fashionable, introducing also the doctrine of 'art for art's sake' in England, were Walter Pater and Oscar Wilde.

Walter Pater (1839–94) came to prominence via a volume of essays entitled *The Renaissance*, first published in 1873, but while his celebrated essay on

Leonardo da Vinci and his often quoted analysis of *Mona Lisa*, whom he described as being 'older than the rocks among which she sits, like the vampire, she has been dead many times, and learned the secrets of the grave' (Pater, 1961, p. 123), are well known to every student of art history, his less well-known essay on Winckelmann reveals his inspiration within the Greek classical ideals of beauty.

Entitled simply 'Winckelmann', this essay was written in 1877, later than his other essays on the Renaissance mostly completed between 1870–72. In it Pater started with Winckelmann's biography, followed by an analysis of his writings, starting with his first book *Thoughts on the Imitation of Greek Works of Art in Painting and Sculpture*, after which he departed for Rome, where he was fortunate to meet one of the foremost collectors of antiquities, Cardinal Albani, who in 1858 became his patron. But Pater makes a curious point regarding Winckelmann's undisputed 'affinity' with the Hellenic spirit, which revealed – as also pointed out by Kenneth Clark in his introduction for the 1961 edition – the nature of Pater's own self-identification with Greek art:

> The hunger for a golden age, the austere devotion to physical beauty, the feeling of a dedication to art and to the unravelling of its laws, 'the desire' as Pater say 'to escape from abstract theory to intuitions, to exercise of sight and touch' – all the characteristics which Winckelmann had united with a burning clarity, Pater recognized as half-smothered fires in his own being. Even those elements in Winckelmann's character which seem more questionable, his formal acceptance of the Catholic faith as the price of a ticket to Rome, and his passionate love affairs with young men, corresponded to impulses which Pater felt in his own character and increased his feelings of sympathy (Clark in Pater, 1961, p. 13).

Although Baudelaire's name is not mentioned, Pater not only reveals a familiarity with his definition of beauty, consisting of a universal and a transient (historical) dimension, but alters it and adopts it as his own:

> Again, individual genius works ever under conditions of time and place: its products are coloured by the varying aspects of nature, and type of human form, and outward manners of life. There is thus an element of change in art; criticism must never for a moment forget that 'the artist is the child of his time'. But besides these conditions of time and place, and independent of them, there is also an element of permanence, a standard of taste, which genius confesses (Pater, 1961, p. 195).

This 'standard of taste' – which Pater may well have borrowed from David Hume's essay of the same title published in 1757 (with which he would undoubtedly have been familiar), 'was fixed in Greece, at a definite historical period' (Pater, 1961, p. 195).

But the main influence at work on Pater's thinking comes from Hegel's aesthetics and explanation of artistic beauty as a vehicle to transcend human finitude in order to approach the absolute or 'godlike', and more specifically from his art history and his division of artistic styles into symbolic, classical and Romantic, each corresponding to one of the arts that Hegel chose to analyse: architecture, sculpture, painting, music and poetry. On this occasion Pater specifically references Hegel's 'The Art of Egypt', with its supreme architectural effects, according to Hegel's beautiful comparison, a 'Memnon waiting for the day, the day of the Greek spirit, the humanistic spirit, with its power of speech' (Pater, 1961, p. 203) and that Greek spirit manifested itself in sculpture. Pater quotes a passage from Hegel, which sums up the Greek 'spirit' and its embodiment in sculpture:

This sense for the consummate modelling of divine and human forms was pre-eminently at home in Greece. In its poets and orators, its historians and philosophers, Greece cannot be conceived from a central point, unless one brings, as a key to the understanding of it, an insight into the ideal forms of sculpture, and regards the images of statesmen and philosophers as well as epic and dramatic heroes, from the artistic point of view (Hegel quoted by Pater, 1961, p. 209).

From this very Hegelian perspective, Pater moves to Winckelmann, saying simply that 'the key to the understanding of the Greek spirit, Winckelmann possessed in his own nature, itself like a relic of classical antiquity, laid open by accident to our alien, modern atmosphere'. More importantly Pater argued 'To his criticism of that consummate Greek modelling he brought not only his culture but his temperament' (Pater, 1961, p. 210).

But then, Pater turned critic, by underlining from his Hegelian perspective what he considered Winckelmann's limitations, as lacking the ability to understand conflict, which emerged already in the serene classical world of Greece with tragedy, pain and sorrow, and his analysis of art did not take on board modernity either. Pater puts this so beautifully that it should have become as famous and as often quoted as his celebrated description of *Mona Lisa*:

Into this stage of Greek achievement Winckelmann did not enter. Supreme as he is where his true interest lay, his insight into the typical unity and repose of the highest sort of sculptures seems to have involved limitation in another direction. His conception of art excludes that bolder type of it which deals confidently and serenely with life, conflict, evil. Living in a world of exquisite but abstract and colourless form, he could hardly have conceived of the subtle and penetrative, yet somewhat grotesque art of the modern world (Pater, 1961, p. 212).

Thus Winckelmann did not manage – Pater argued like a good Hegelian – to absorb the higher order 'Christian Romantic' art, but somebody else did: Johann Wolfgang von Goethe (1749–1832) who, unlike Winkelmann, was steeped in the Romanticism of his time. Pater argued that for Goethe, the problem was 'can the blitheness and universality of the antique ideal be communicated to artistic productions, which shall contain the fullness of the experience of the modern world?' (Pater, 1961, p. 217). Pater's answer was that of Hegel: it was possible, because of the dialectical development of art, which found its correspondence in that of the human mind (*geist*): 'Sculpture corresponds to the unperplexed, emphatic outlines of Hellenic humanism; painting to the mystic depth and intricacy of the middle age; music and poetry have their fortune in the modern world' (Pater, 1961, pp. 217–18).

Thus Goethe and Victor Hugo's Romantic writings belong to modern art, dealing with modern life, while Winkelmann, whose passion for sculpture retarded him academically and emotionally, stayed in the Hellenistic past.

Oscar Wilde's genius

As a creative writer, Oscar Wilde (1854–1900) took a different route to the doctrine of 'art for art's sake' from Pater, who nonetheless influenced him profoundly. It was also his passion for beauty that attracted him to its most immediate and direct public manifestation: fashion, and he became the first 'fashion journalist'. His journalistic activities are less well known than his artistic input, but they are important, not only because they reveal a different aspect of his creativity, but also because they reveal Oscar Wilde as an astute observer and critic of Victorian society. He could pursue his journalistic interests as the editor of the magazine *The Woman's World*, a position he held for two years. One of the most interesting manifestations of his socialism was his attitude towards the emancipation of women, and to that effect a number of relevant articles were published in the magazine. Among them was a fascinating article signed by Laura M'Laren entitled 'On the Fallacy of the Superiority of Men', in which the author demolishes one by one all stereotype arguments against equality between men and women by arguing that it is in fact a matter of education, politics and society which keeps women from becoming achievers. She concludes with a remarkable paragraph worth quoting for its prophetic content: 'If by the year 1987 the position of women in the artistic, musical, scientific and literary worlds is not equal to that of the other sex in their day, men will then be able to write a plausible essay on the inherent inferiority of women' (M'Laren, 1887, pp. 54–6).

The magazine provided also a platform for Oscar Wilde's interest in fashion, by enabling him to publish numerous articles on the subject.

In the volume of Oscar Wilde's 'Complete Works', his son Vyvyan wrote in his introduction, 'The most interesting essay in the book is *The Decay of Lying*. The essay is in the form of a dialogue, the dominant theme being the vast superiority of Art over Nature, leading to the conclusion that nature follows Art' (Holland in Wilde, 1968, p. 12).

The essay is indeed a dialogue between Oscar Wilde's two sons, Vyvyan and Cyril, and it is the former who outlines the primacy of art over nature and its process of decay when that relationship is altered:

Art begins with abstract decoration, with purely imaginative and pleasurable work dealing with what is unreal and non-existent. This is the first stage. Then Life becomes fascinated with this new wonder, and asks to be admitted into the charmed circle. Art takes life as part of her rough material, recreates it, and refashions it in fresh forms, is absolutely indifferent to fact, invents, imagines, dreams and keeps between herself and reality the impenetrable barrier of beautiful style, of decorative or ideal treatment. The third stage is when Life gets the upper hand, and drives Art out into the wilderness. This is the rue decadence, and it is from this that we are now suffering (Wilde, 1968, p. 978).

At the end of the dialogue, Vyvyan outlines to Cyril the three doctrines of his new aesthetics:

1. Art never expresses anything but itself. It has an independent life, just as Thought has, and develops purely on its on lines . . . 2. All bad art comes from returning to Life and Nature, and elevating them into ideals. Life and Nature may sometimes be used as part of Art's rough material but before they are of nay real service to Art they must be translated into artistic conventions . . . 3. Life imitates Art far more than Art imitates Life. This results not merely from Life's imitative instinct, but from the fact that the self-conscious aim of Life is to find expression, and that Art offers it certain beautiful forms through which it may realise that energy (Wilde, 1968, pp. 991–2).

Oscar Wilde introduced his new aesthetics in the preface of his best known novel, *The Picture of Dorian Gray*, proclaiming its independence and self-sufficiency:

The artist is the creator of beautiful things.
To reveal art and conceal the artist is art's aim.
The critic is he who can translate into another manner or a new material his impression of beautiful things.

The highest, as the lowest, form of criticism is a mode of autobiography.

Those who find ugly meanings in beautiful things are corrupt without being charming. This is a fault.

Those who find beautiful meanings in beautiful things are the cultivated. For these there is hope.

They are the elect to whom beautiful things mean only Beauty.

There is no such thing as a moral or an immoral book.

Books are well written, or badly written. That is all (Wilde, 1968, p. 17).

In the novel Oscar Wilde referenced one such book dealing with beauty, whose content was as far removed from any issues pertaining to morality: Joris-Karl Huysmans' famous *A Rebours*, translated into English as *Against Nature*. Dorian Gray's friend Lord Henry Wotton sent him a book whose fascination haunted him for years to come, and Oscar Wilde captured the moment when Dorian Gray fell under its mysterious spell: 'His eyes fell on the yellow book that Lord Henry had sent him. What was it, he wondered . . . It was the strangest book that he had ever read . . . Things that he had dimly dreamed of were suddenly made real to him. Things of which he had never dreamed were gradually revealed' (Wilde, 1968, p. 101).

Indeed, the book written by fellow critic Karl-Joris Huysmans (1848–1907), came to be regarded as the 'keystone of the so-called Decadence, that movement in France and England characterized by a delight in the perverse and the artificial'.

Huysmans' followers included Paul Valéry, who made this book his 'bible and bedside book' – not only because it mirrored their 'decadent' ideas and aspirations, but also because it revealed and consecrated a new and exciting literature, the literature of Baudelaire, Verlaine and Mallarmé (Baldick in Huysmans, 1971, Introduction; see also Furbank and Cain, 2004). From the first pages Huysmans throws open a provocation: the eponymous hero, Duc Jean Floressas Des Esseintes, gave a dinner party to 'mark the most ludicrous of personal misfortunes', the loss of his virility, and this banquet modelled on an eighteenth-century original and described in great detail is a foretaste of things to come; Huysmans did not disappoint. The dining room opened onto a garden whose paths had been strewn with charcoal, the pond edged with black basalt, and the shrubberies replanted with cypresses and pines. The dinner itself however was the *pièce de resistance:*

While a hidden orchestra played funeral marches, the guests were waited on by naked negresses wearing only slippers and stockings in cloth of silver embroidered with tears. Dining off black-bordered plates, the company had enjoyed turtle soup, Russian rye bread, ripe olives from Turkey, caviare, mullet botargo, black puddings from Frankfurt, game served in sauces the colour of liquorice and boot-polish, truffle jellies, chocolate creams, plum-puddings, nectarines, pears in grape-juice syrup, mulberries, and black heart-cherries. From dark-tinted glasses they had drunk the wines of Limagne and Roussillon, of Tenedos, Valdepeñas and Oporto. And after coffee and walnut cordial, they had rounded off the evening with kvass, porter, and stout (Huysmans, 1971, p. 27).

What is less commented about the book is Huysmans' impressive expertise as an art critic, revealed on several occasions when he embarked on critical analysis of works by Gustave Moreau and Odilon Redon, which his character (based on the Comte de Montesquiou) 'Des Esseintes' collected. A typical decadent and ambiguous Redon may be viewed here.

The two paintings by Gustave Moreau that he owned were *Salomé* and a water-colour entitled *The Apparition*, dedicated to the same subject. After commenting on the erotic subject matter, Huysmans mused over the qualities of water-colour as a medium:

It was Des Esseintes' opinion that never before, in any period, had the art of water-colour produced such brilliant hues; never before had an aquarellist's wretched chemical pigments been able to make paper sparkle so brightly with precious stones, shine so colourfully with sunlight filtered through stained-glass windows, glitter so splendidly with sumptuous garments, glow so warmly with exquisite flesh-tints (Huysmans, 1971, p. 69).

As for Odilon Redon, whose drawings Des Esseintes considered to 'defy classification', Huysmans provided a very good analysis, revealing Redon's twin inspiration from botanical and scientific drawings and from the world of dreams:

Sometimes Redon's subjects actually seemed to be borrowed from the nightmares of science, to go back to prehistoric times: a monstrous flora spread over the rocks, and among the ubiquitous boulders and glacier mud-streams wandered bipeds whose apish features – the heavy jaws, the protruding brows, the receding forehead, the flattened top of the skull – recalled the head of our ancestors early in the Quaternary Period, when man was still fructivorous and speechless, a contemporary of the mammoth, the woolly rhinoceros, and the cave-bear (Huysman, 1971, p. 73).

From a position of an adherent to the 'art for art's sake', Huysmans would have had little sympathy for the dour moralizing of Denis Diderot as the critic of the eighteenth-century *salon*, and we find Des Esseintes being dismissive of him and his fellow Encyclopedists:

Figure 9 Odilon Redon, *And his name that sat on the pale horse was Death (. . . et celui que était monté dessus se nommait la Mort . . .)*, 1899, lithograph on *chine collé*, 31.2 × 22.6 cm (image), National Gallery of Victoria, Melbourne, Gift of James Mollison AO, 1991.

As for prose, he had little respect for Voltaire and Rousseau, or even for Diderot, whose vaunted 'Salons' struck him as remarkable for the number of moralizing inanities and stupid aspirations they contained. Out of hatred of all this twaddle, he confined his reading almost entirely to the exponents of Christian oratory, to Bourdaloue and Bossuet, whose sonorous and ornate periods greatly impressed him (Huysmans, 1971, p. 148).

'Ethics' and 'morality' versus' art' and 'aesthetics'

Definitions of art are as multiple and diverse as there are forms of art, but we are all agreed that a working definition of the kind found in a dictionary provides a useful starting point. One such is: 'the creation of works of beauty or other special significance' or 'the products of man's creative activities: works of art collectively, especially of the visual arts, sometimes also music, drama, dance, and literature' (*Collins English Dictionary*, 2005, p. 89). There are plenty of other variations on the theme available, but essentially art has to do with a special kind of activity. Things are less clear with the matter of 'morality', however, and for that reason, instead of a dictionary, we turn to the distinguished philosopher Bernard Williams, who defined moral philosophy thus: 'Moral philosophy is the philosophical reflective study of certain values that concern human beings. A sense of ethical values informs people's lives, directly in deciding what to do, and in their comments and judgements on people and actions including their own' (Williams in Grayling, 1995, p. 546).

There is a distinction between the terms *ethics* and *morality* often used interchangeably, although they are not synonyms: the former is derived from the Greek word *ethos* ('personal character'), which 'carries a broader conception, including a concern with the value of different kinds of life and activity', while the Latin word *moralia* ('social custom', which provides also the root for the word *moda*, 'fashion') narrows down its meaning to 'rules and obligations, and to the experience and considerations most closely related to those' (Williams in Grayling, 1995, p. 546).

The moot question to be addressed is: can art and/or aesthetics be understood without reference to morality, or are they intrinsically linked? Two distinct positions corresponding to the two 'doctrines' of 'art for art's sake' and 'art for morality's sake' prevail, which can be summarized as follows:

- We are dealing with two autonomous domains.

- There is a conceptual link between them which can be traced at least as far back as Immanuel Kant and Friedrich Schiller, both of whom hold the view that the beautiful is the symbol of the morally good.

Twentieth-century philosophers tend to regard art as an autonomous subject and aesthetics as an autonomous academic discipline, and this position is perfectly summed up by Stuart Hampshire's comment that 'the enjoyment of art, and art itself, is . . . a detached and peculiar pleasure, which leads to nothing else. Its part in the whole experience of man is then left unexplained' (quoted by White in Cooper, 1995, p. 295). But while his laconic statement appears to be no more than the kind of philosophical 'shoulder shrugging' we encounter with all great metaphysicians who do not take philosophical aesthetics too seriously, this was not the case during the nineteenth century, when the phrase *l'art pour l'art* (art for art's sake) became the rallying cry of the Aesthetic movement. It is important to emphasize here that the Romantic attitude towards the purity of aesthetic experience was launched first by a group of writers. The movement was primarily associated with three of them: Théophile Gautier (1811–72), Charles Baudelaire (1821–67) and Gustave Flaubert (1821–80), who provided the confirmation of Aestheticism, yet its theoretical inception has been traced to a philosopher, Victor Cousin (1792–1867), whose series of lectures entitled 'The True, the Beautiful and the Good', delivered at the Sorbonne, were subsequently published as a book in 1837 (Harrison, Wood, Gaiger, 2000, p. 192).

We find Cousin arguing in favour of an independent art (Lecture VIII), although he did not see the need to isolate it by separating it:

> from religion, from morals, from country. Art draws its inspiration from these profound sources, as well as from the ever open source of nature. But it is not less true that art, the state, religion, are powers which have each their world apart and their own effects; they mutually help each other; they should not serve each other. As soon as one of them wanders from its end, it errs, and is degraded. Does art blindly give itself up to the orders of religion and the state? In losing its liberty, it loses its charm and its empire (Cousin in Harrison, Wood, Gaiger, 2000, pp. 192–3).

In Lecture IX two important issues are addressed: first the final cause (*telos*) of art, which is the 'beautiful'. Cousin puts it so simply and eloquently: 'The sole object of art is the beautiful. Art abandons itself as soon as it shuns this' (Harrison, Wood, Gaiger, 2000, p. 196). Cousin also brings into focus the different means by which each form of art achieves the same end: the 'beautiful', and at this point he is referring to the celebrated essay 'Laocoön', by Gotthold Ephraim Lessing (1792–81). Written in 1766, 'Laocoön or The Limits of Painting and Poetry' is considered as one of the most important essays in literary criticism. In it, Lessing undertook to establish the interstices between poetry and painting as his choice of examples, arguing that each form of art has its intrinsic limitations which need to be understood and respected.

Lessing was interested in Winckelmann's evaluation of the celebrated sculpture *Laocoön* for one important reason: to analyse how pain is expressed in a sculpture and then parallel it with a literary description, and for that he chose Virgil's *Aeneid*. Laocoön was a Trojan priest who allegedly offended the god Poseidon and in revenge he sent two giant sea serpents to kill him and his two sons. This is the subject of both the sculpture and (with variations) the myth. The theme of the sculpture is extreme human suffering, and the question of how it could be expressed in artistic form constituted the core of Lessing's argument, as well as his argument that it dated from the time of Alexander the Great.

The finest expression of how the physical embodiment of the concept of ideal beauty can be represented visually in all its purity without being spoilt by any emotion comes from Charles Baudelaire's celebrated poem, 'La Beauté' in *Les Fleurs du mal*:

Je hais le moveument qui déplace les lignes,
Et jamais je ne pleure et jamais je ne ris
[translated by James McGowan as follows]:
I hate only impulse, the breaking of line,
And I never will cry, nor will ever show smile (Baudelaire, 1998, pp. 38–9).

Instead of considering the aesthetic experience as an end in itself, Tolstoy regarded it as a means towards an end, which consisted first in the transmission of the artist's emotions to his audience, and second, once this was achieved, to attain a 'brotherhood of men', which was a Christian brotherhood to Tolstoy.

Tolstoy's model of a transmitter or receiver according to which the artist incorporates his emotions in his work of art, becoming the vehicle to transmit those very emotions to the audience, aligned it to 'the expression theory of art', primarily associated with Benedetto Croce and R.G. Collinwood, is considered to have originated with the English and European Romantic poets 'and its rudiments were first set out by Tolstoy, for whom art serves as a vehicle for transmitting morally purposive emotion' (Gardner in Grayling, 1995, p. 616).

Tolstoy calls this process 'infection', arguing that the spectators or auditors 'are infected' by the feelings which the author has felt, and he then argued somewhat in a circle, that if this condition is fulfilled only then do we have a work of art:

To evoke in oneself a feeling one has once experienced, and having evoked it in oneself, then, by means of movements, lines, colours, sounds, or forms expressed in words, so to transmit that feeling that others may experience the same feeling – this is the activity of art. Art is a human activity consisting in this, that one man consciously, by means of certain external signs, hands on to others feeling he has lived through, and that other people are infected by these feelings and also experience them (Tolstoy in Feagin and Maynard, 1997, pp. 170–1).

The second point made by Tolstoy provides a critical criterion for what might account for 'good art', and that can only be Christian art, because it promotes 'the brotherhood of man' and this Christian art:

> should be catholic in the original meaning of the word, that is, universal, and therefore it should unite all men. And only two kinds of feeling unite all men; first feelings flowing from our sonship to God and of the brotherhood of man; and next, the simple feelings of common life accessible to every one without exception – such as feelings of merriment, of pity, of cheerfulness, of tranquillity, and so forth. Only these two kinds of feelings can now supply material for art good in its subject-matter (Tolstoy quoted by Sorrell in Hanfling, 1992, p. 315).

Tolstoy then embarked on an evaluative exercise and by using Christian art as his critical criterion reaches the monumental conclusion that there is very little good religious art. Among the novels and authors he approved of were Victor Hugo's *Les Misérables* and Charles Dickens's *A Tale of Two Cities*, with additions by George Eliot, Dostoevsky, Schiller and Tolstoy's own short story 'God Sees the Truth but Waits', but he dismissed his major novels as bad art; the superlative examples come from antiquity, specifically the Bible, with the story of Joseph topping the chart (Sorell in Hanfling, 1992).

Nor does what Tolstoy labelled the category of 'imitation arts' – by which he meant 'the thousands of 'paintings, musical pieces and novels by run-of-the-mill professional painters, composers and writers but also a number of works generally reckoned great, such as Shakespeare's *Hamlet*, Beethoven's sonata Opus 101 and Wagner's *Ring* (Sorrell in Hanfling, 1992, p. 317) – fare better. The reason is that although they evoke strong emotions, they are the wrong ones, for instead of promoting 'the brotherhood of man' they are likely to 'evoke sexual desire or feelings of horror' (Sorrell in Hanfling, 1992, p. 317).

Tolstoy is equally critical of art that is not universally accessible, and he attacked not only the artists but also the critics and art dealers who promoted it, and to that effect makes a wonderful point that art need not necessarily be what we have traditionally been accustomed to: 'We are accustomed to understand art to be only what we hear and see in theatres, concerts, and exhibitions, together with buildings, statues, poems, novels . . . But all this is but the smallest part of the art by which we communicate with each other in life' (Tolstoy in Feagin and Maynard, 1997, p. 171).

If we define art as a vehicle of communication through which the artist 'infects' his audience in a very special way, which has less to do with aesthetic pleasure and more to do with moral purposes, then it is possible to consider that we need not look at Shakespeare or even Dickens, and Tolstoy said as much when he argued that these are only the smallest part of the art defined in the narrow sense established by canons, through which we communicate:

> All human life is filled with works of art of every kind – from cradlesong, jest, mimicry, the ornamentation of houses, dress, and utensils, up to church services, buildings, monuments and triumphal processions. It is all artistic activity. So that by art, in the limited sense of the word, we do not mean all human activity transmitting feelings, but only that art which we for some reason select from it and to which we attach special importance. This special importance has always been given by all men to that part of this activity which transmits feelings flowing from their religious perception, and this small part of art they have specifically called art, attaching to it the full meaning of the word (Tolstoy in Feagin and Maynard, 1997, p. 171).

In *The Literate Eye: Victorian Art Writing and Modernist Aesthetics*, Rachel Teukolsky argues, 'Nineteenth-century British writers helped to invent an idea new in the nineteenth century, that art spectatorship could provide one of the most intense and meaningful forms of human experience' (Teukolsky, 2009, p. 3). She suggests that Anglo-American art criticism of this time enabled the development of 'the moves towards formalism and abstraction that would come to dominate twentieth-century canons of art and value' (Teukolsky, 2009, p. 3). This was a culture that was driving towards a more secular worldview. Art writing, then, was not simply a matter of entertainment or erudition, but drove a major cultural shift towards different registers of human creativity. She argues for criticism, 'the cultural history of aesthetic judgments', as mediating the new social forces between producers and consumers (Teukolsky, 2009, p. 6). There was also a place for fashion within this new worldview.

PART TWO

REPORTING FASHION

OVERVIEW

Figure 10 Photographer's proof sheet for *Harper's Bazaar*, 75th Anniversary, October 1942, Image Courtesy The Museum at the Fashion Institute of Technology, New York, 78.84.375. Photograph by Louise Dahl-Wolfe © 1989 Center for Creative Photography, Arizona Board of Regents.

This part of the book provides an introductory background and a series of examples that analyse the emergence of a judicial (evaluative) vocabulary for fashion journalists. By focusing on primary sources – the writings of professional critics – the reader learns how they 'do their job'.

A case will be made by comparing the descriptive approach of the newly emerging fashion writers in the early twentieth century (mostly women and of non-specialist background, which is significant) with the pioneering approach to art criticism adopted by the *philosophe* Denis Diderot in the eighteenth century. No canon for evaluating public art existed prior to Diderot, who had to invent his own, and this he did with his reviews of the *salons*, discussed in Part 1 of this book. The reviews of the *salons* amounted to no more than description, albeit of great elegance and irony, of the paintings on display. Yet, aware of his 'mission', Diderot also provided a modest evaluative vocabulary, which was based on the four major categories of fine art: composition, drawing, colour and expression, as stipulated by Louis Testelin (1615–55), commissioned by Louis XIV to draw the synoptic tables of the Rules for Great Art, for the newly found Royal Academy of Painting and Sculpture. Diderot's celebrated *Salons* thus provided the template for the emergence of the first 'professional' art critic, Charles Baudelaire, who, a century later as the art critic nominated to report on the *salons* in the press, invented his own evaluative term: *modernité*. Thus the first art critics deployed terminologies from philosophy and poetry respectively to write about art and (in the case of Baudelaire to provide the first evaluative term in the history of fashion criticism, borrowed from his magisterial *Les fleurs du mal*, '*charme*'). Therefore, in this part of the book, we connect early modern, nineteenth- and twentieth-century concepts of evaluation as they concerned fashion reporting for the twentieth century.

Continuities of critical writing such as the notion 'to be *de bon ton*' are explored across two centuries. In the first years of the twentieth century not just the quality of writing changed, but a radical change occurred in the way the page was presented, including typography and illustrations, creating a new impetus for understanding fashion. For example, the development of luxurious *pochoir* fashion illustrations created by Paul Iribe and Georges Lepape for the *Gazette du bon ton* revolutionized the traditional fashion illustration; they replaced the simple reproduction of garments with *tableaux-vivants* that depicted stylish and chic daily life as well as fantasy.

Concerning the 'snapshots'

The issue under consideration at this point of the book is *fashion reporting*. The preferred mode of reporting (from the moment couture houses came into existence during the second half of the nineteenth century) was to visit them in

LA PANTOUFLE DE VAIR

Danseur Louis XIV

Gazette du Bon Ton. — Nº 4   Février 1913. — Pl. 1

Figure 11 A.E. Marty, illustrator, *La Pantoufle de Vair, Danseur Louis XIV* ['The fur slipper, Louis XIV dancer' a pun in French on the translation of fur and glass – the former 'vair' and the latter 'verre'], drawn 1912, published in *Gazette du Bon Ton*, no. 4, Plate 1, February 1913, *pochoir* print, collection of Peter McNeil.

person and create a narrative for readers. The style of writing was mostly descriptive commentary about the new collections on display and what could be seen at the main *maisons de couture* in Paris, whose unchallenged domination was reflected through and within the nascent critical terminology used to evaluate them. Terms such as *charm, grace, elegance* and *glamour*, which started to be employed in an *evaluative* manner for these reports, were subsequently adopted internationally, so that we find them in American and European magazines, and all the way to the Balkans. Parisian fashion magazines therefore provided the template for the global span of fashion reporting, co-extensive with the imperialist expansion of French *haute couture*, a fact that is little noted by historians and commentators. This enables our project to have relevance far beyond the Franco–English axis that dominates much fashion scholarship. This part of the book therefore is innovative in that it does not suggest that fashion reporting is trivial, but in fact was founded on a long tradition of evaluative and critical writing that is historically specific and has both benefits and limitations for the assessment of fashion clothing.

In the thematic category we examine the origins of concepts relating to values and criticism and then analyse their relevance today. Thus the debate 'art for art's sake' and 'art and morality' extends back to Charles Baudelaire, Oscar Wilde and so on, who considered that art was solely for aesthetic pleasure (Langlade, 1997, Introduction). Others suggested that morality was the highest aim: the views of Leo Tolstoy and John Ruskin on artistic endeavour also colour many subsequent understandings of fashion. An example of our intention in this section follows: Socratic irony is a delightful rhetorical tool that goes back to ancient Greek literature, whereby the opposite of what is meant is stated; or more recently, 'less' than what is meant is stated; the famous 'understatement' of the fashion world, filled with monumental egos often accompanied by ignorance (the etymology of the word 'irony' is 'feigning ignorance', something that Socrates used regularly). This can be a lethal critical tool that is also venerable regarding its origins.

SNAPSHOTS

Fashion and morality: Leo Tolstoy: *what is art*?

Leo Tolstoy (1828–1910) better known for his celebrated novels, such as *Anna Karenina* and *War and Peace*, was also interested in philosophy, religion, politics; in other words, he was a polymath and his curiosity attracted him to religion, politics and philosophy, specifically two subjects – aesthetics and ethics – which Tolstoy argued were intrinsically linked. To that effect he wrote an essay he entitled 'What is Art?', first published in 1896. Tolstoy's argument that the only art worth having is an art that can be justified on moral grounds must be understood against the emergence of the French doctrine *l'art pour l'art*, translated into English as 'art for art's sake', which emerged in literary criticism, first in the writings of the French poets and writers such as Charles Baudelaire, Théophile Gautier and Gustave Flaubert. Put simply, it proposes that art is an end in itself, and therefore must be free of any other preoccupation such as morality, politics, propaganda or educational purposes. Its *telos* (final cause) therefore is the disinterested pleasure required in the aesthetic experience.

Against this doctrine, Tolstoy argued that if so much effort and time went into creating art, then art could not possibly be separated from religious or moral purposes, as in the example of medieval art. He creates a linear link between art and beauty: art – there is no definition of art – art is that which makes beauty manifest; beauty is that which is pleasing (without exciting desire), by which Tolstoy means the 'disinterested' pleasure first postulated by the Third Earl of Shaftesbury as a necessary condition for the aesthetic experience. Tolstoy rejected this position, which sums up the essence of the French doctrine of 'art for art's sake', replacing it with an 'expression theory' of art, whereby there is a link, which he quaintly called 'infection', between artists and their audience: artists become the transmitter of their personal experience through their artistic endeavour; the audience becomes the receiver of that experience and the message is the work of art: 'To evoke in oneself a feeling one has once experienced, and having evoked it in oneself, then, by means of movements, lines, colours, sounds, or forms expressed in words, so to transmit that feeling that other may experience the same feeling – this is the activity of art' (Tolstoy in Feagin and Maynard, 1997, p. 170).

From this Tolstoy derived his other important doctrine, that of the 'Christian brotherhood of man', whereby the value of each work of art corresponds with the highest religious perception of that age, which was Tolstoy's own age. That could mean only the late-nineteenth century, which should be idealistically dominated by the 'Christian ideal of the union and brotherhood of man', but this was not the truth.

Nothing less would do, and Tolstoy provided a list of authors and works of art that fall short of his two criteria, which included not only Shakespeare and Michelangelo, but also his own novels. To try to link Tolstoy to fashion writing would be futile, but not so his passion for morality, for exactly a century later, the 1990s brought with them an awareness of issues such as climate change, AIDS and pressure on global resources, which started to make the headlines in the press, pointing to the negative aspects of globalization, capitalism and its ruthless exploitation of our poor planet. The fashion world was quick to react in its own way by publicly (at least) rejecting its image of excess, bling and the Thatcherite Yuppies, and embracing everything to do with preservation, conservation, recycling, upcycling and minimalism, whose new heroes included Martin Margiela's 'deconstruction' clothes and 'situationist' fashion shows, and the Japanese contingent, which brought to Europe a new awareness of craft, so dear to the likes of Leo Tolstoy and John Ruskin a century before.

Moreover, we now see the emergence of *ethical fashion*, with all its attendant issues such as recycling, vintage fashion and the environment (never more relevant than in the present climate), just like *ethical medicine* and *ethical journalism* have been addressing such issues from their specific perspectives before it. There is, however, another way of addressing fashion by linking it with ethics, whereby instead of ethical fashion, the philosophical discipline of ethics is linked to the world of fashion: instead of 'ethical fashion' we have 'ethics and fashion'.

Ethics or moral philosophy is a branch of philosophy which deals with the study of certain values that concern human beings and the understanding of certain kinds of reason for human action, and how we make decisions about them: 'what ought I to do' in any given situation becomes the central preoccupation of ethics. Given that it deals with human action, ethics more than any other philosophical subject overlaps (as pointed out by the British philosopher Bernard Williams) with other subjects outside philosophy, noticeably politics, medicine, journalism and the law, so it is possible to talk about 'applied ethics', whereby we can use ethics as a tool to deal with other issues of human concern. Fashion and ethics are yet to be linked in this way and we intend to use the argument from analogy in order to try and postulate just such a link.

The simple question to be posed here is whether it is morally right or wrong to 'resurrect' or 'reinvent' a 'dead' label for commercial gain, as in the recent examples of Madeleine Vionnet and Elsa Schiaparelli (among many others). The argument will centre on a comparison with an example taken from sculpture, that of the *surmoulage*. For instance, how would Umberto Boccioni's four posthumous bronze casts of his sculpture entitled *Unique Forms of Continuity in Space* be regarded in the sense of what kind of status they can claim? Are they related to an original?, a copy?; or should we postulate a new category: the *surmoulage*, which would create a new price tag for the benefit of Christie's and Sotheby's? In the same way, what would we call a 'Schiaparelli' dress made in 2009 and not by Schiaparelli? The marketplace appears to have already decided.

Paul Poiret: 'Sultan of fashion' – from tradition to innovation

In the early twentieth century Paul Poiret (1879–1944), the most celebrated couturier in the period of the First World War, used a slightly different notion of pre-empting what clients already wanted: 'I respond to your hidden intentions by anticipating them.' Not just a sultan or just a king: Paul Poiret aimed much higher when he declared that fashion 'needs a tyrant' and he was that tyrant. His life straddled the nineteenth and twentieth centuries and for that reason history was on his side, by creating the enabling circumstances for him to perform the radical transition from tradition to innovation by ushering Modernism into fashion.

The advent of the twentieth century was marked in Paris by the heroic *Exposition Universelle* of 1900, which marked the *apogée* of the pleasure-seeking period that came to be known as *La Belle Epoque*, whose opulent frivolity found its most sophisticated expression in fashion. There were flounces, feathers, lace, plumage, *strass* and above all the erotic 'S' curve, all of which became the target of Paul Poiret's campaign of freeing women from its tyranny by waging war against the corset, crinoline and bustle.

Apart from its breath-taking grandeur, the exhibition had a special significance for *haute couture* through the pioneering introduction of a pavilion dedicated to fashion: the *Chambre syndicale de la confection pour dames et enfants* organized an exhibition under the title *Les toilettes de la collectivité de la couture*, which incorporated the twenty most important couture houses in Paris (Mendes and de la Haye, 1999).

The phenomenon that came to be known as *haute couture* had just emerged on the Parisian fashion scene when the English born *couturier*, Charles Frederick Worth (1825–95), opened the first *maison de couture*; Jacques Doucet (1853–1929) opened the second soon afterwards. Worth and Doucet were Paul Poiret's first employers, with whom he learnt the rudiments of his craft, after which, in 1903 – with a little help from his mother – he opened his own *maison de couture* at 5, rue Auber. But being just a maker of clothes was not enough; Poiret aspired to be an artist, as he famously declared in his autobiography, first published in 1930, which he entitled with characteristic panache *En habillent l'époque (Dressing the Era)*. In it he famously declared: 'Am I a fool when I dream of putting art into my dresses, a fool when I say dressmaking is an art? For I have always loved painters and felt on an equal footing with them. It seems to me that we practice the same craft' (Montebello in Koda and Bolton, 2007). Whether fashion can be regarded as art continues to be a matter of debate, but one thing is certain: Poiret not only befriended some of the leading *avant-garde* artists starting with the two radical art movements that emerged at the beginning of the twentieth century, Fauvism and Cubism, but he collaborated with them. Their influence became evident in the way he introduced the vivid colours that caused the critic Louis Vauxcelles in 1905 to deride Henri Matisse and his fellow painters who were exhibiting at the *Salon d'automne*, calling them 'wild beasts' (*fauves*), and more dramatically at a structural level. Poiret was the first modern couturier to replace the fitted with the draped system predominant during classical antiquity and whose importance cannot be overemphasized: 'Poiret's process of design through draping is the source of fashion's modern forms' (Koda and Bolton, 2007, p. 14).

It was also the influence of the Cubists and their use of prismatic faceting in building volume on the flat surface of a painting that inspired Poiret to flatten the silhouette (Martin, 1998). Specifically Poiret ushered Modernism into fashion through a succession of prodigious styles starting with his first original collection inspired by the *directoire* style, which in turn revolutionized fashion in the aftermath of the French Revolution by replacing the ornate rococo style – which symbolized the excesses of the totalitarian French monarchy – with the severe neo-classical silhouette, inspired by the democratic Greek *chiton*. This was followed by the Orientalist phase for Poiret, where the influence of the *Ballets russes*, especially their exotic and colourful costumes designed by Léon Bakst – the likes of which had never seen before 1909 when the *Saisson russe* was premiered in Paris with several ballets. Under their influence, Poiret embarked on his Orientalist phase, by daring to put women in harem pants, lampshade tunics and turbans decorated with exotic plumage whose wild extravagance created a veritable sensation. But Poiret did even better than just dressing his affluent clientele in outfits out of *1001 Nights*: he pioneered a new approach to fashion illustration, fashion photography and furniture and interior design, the perfume industry, and as if this were not enough, his *soirées* and balls became at least as well publicized as the performances of the *Ballets russes*. Thus in 1911, he organized a carefully publicized themed ball that he called The Thousand and Second Night, one year after the success of the ballet *Schéhérezade*, whose daring costumes and set designs by Léon Bakst took Paris by storm.

Poiret's two other enterprises were undertaken in collaboration with his daughters, one Martine, with whom he opened a decorative arts school and workshop: *École and Maison Martine* inaugurated in 1911, under the influence of the Wiener Werkstätte initiated in 1903 by Koloman Moser. The second was in collaboration with his daughter Rosine, *Les Parfums de Rosine*, 'the first perfume and cosmetics firm founded by a couturier' (Silver in Koda and Bolton, 2007, p. 47).

The First World War (1914–18) brought to an abrupt end *La Belle Epoque* as well as Paul Poiret's vertiginous success and the Europe that emerged in its aftermath was very different from the easy going and optimistic first decade of the twentieth century. Poiret was not defeated, but overtaken, and by 1929 at the close of his business, he could no longer compete with the streamlined aesthetics of the machine age. He retired to the South of France and spent his last year painting, but Paul Poiret's legacy as the first truly modernist couturier of the twentieth century remains intact.

Diana Vreeland: 'Why don't you?' – the invention of the fashion editor[1]

Where would fashion be without literature?

Vreeland, 1984, p. 82.

Diana Vreeland (Mrs T. Reed) (1903–89) was born in Paris. She was wealthy and beautifully dressed, favouring the dresses of Coco Chanel in her youth. Because of her striking personal style she was spotted as a potential magazine writer, joining *Harper's Bazaar* in 1936, in the exciting years of Martin Munkácsi's photographs and Alexey Brodovitch's graphic design, moving to the position of fashion editor there from 1939. She worked extensively with the great fashion photographer Louise Dahl-Wolf, with whom Vreeland acted as stylist and created various mis-en-scènes that developed a particularly dynamic and American vision of fashion (Arnold, 2002, p. 59).

Vreeland finally became editor in chief of *American Vogue* from 1963 until she was terminated in 1971.

Vreeland is infamous for her series of columns 'Why don't you?', which appeared in *Harper's Bazaar* from March 1936. The most infamous is 'Why don't you . . . rinse your blond child's hair in dead champagne to keep its gold, as they do in France?' Others include 'Why don't you . . . order Schiaparelli's cellophane belt with your name and telephone number on it?' and 'Why don't you . . . have a private staircase from your bedroom to the library with a needlework carpet with notes of music worked on each step – the whole spelling your favourite tune?' (here she alluded to the 1930s staircase at West Dean Park with the woven wet footprints of the Austrian-born actress Tilly Losch, later replaced with dog paws). She was quickly satirized, but her concern was fantasy and her milieu was in part

Figure 12 Photographer's proof sheet for *Harper's Bazaar, Christmas Issue*, December 1951, Image Courtesy The Museum at the Fashion Institute of Technology, New York, 78.84.133. Photograph by Louise Dahl-Wolfe © 1989 Center for Creative Photography, Arizona Board of Regents.

Surrealist, '"Why Don't You?" was a thing of fashion and fantasy, on the wing . . . It wasn't writing, it was just ideas. It was me, insisting on people using their imaginations, insisting on a certain idea of luxury' (Stuart, 2012, p. 119).

Vreeland did much to promote the new fashions and attitudes of the post-war period, whether they be Dynel-hair braids, which she loved for their glossy artifice, superstar models posed in exotic mise-en-scènes including one famous spread, which included a beautiful Japanese man ('The West is boring itself to death', she had noted, Vreeland, 1984, p. 52), blue jeans which she admired, and long-legged pop stars. Vreeland was not an intellectual but she loved world culture, atmosphere and civilization. This she brought together in new combinations of word and images in her magazine work, particularly through the double-page spread, commissioning great photographers such as Horst P. Horst to create the first true lifestyle fashions spreads accompanied by erudite and clever prose by his partner, the ex-diplomat Valentine Lawford.

Vreeland appears to have cared very much for the standard of writing in her magazine. In a letter addressed to Mrs Loew Gross (15 November 1967) regarding the feature 'The Romantic Point of View' she stated:

> I think we have words in here that don't belong . . . I am a little let down by this as I see no mention of *Le Grand Meaulnes* [novel published in 1913] and I find the writing not romantic in itself . . . Let us make our writing the very best . . . lets [sic] have it flow and have a rhythm that is essential to the projection of any point as easy and subtle as this one (Vreeland, 2013, p. 21).

At her funeral Richard Avedon said that she 'lived for imagination ruled by discipline and created a totally new profession. Diana Vreeland invented the fashion editor' (Rossi-Camus, 2012, p. 213).

Christian Dior: the 'New Look' and reporting by Carmel Snow

Fashion in the post Second World War period was characterized by mass consumption and production, and the use of man-made fibres. Nonetheless, the luxurious 'New Look' (1947) of Christian Dior (1905–57) is in most minds the iconic style of the time. The sensation of Dior's 'New Look' (which he called the Corolle line) had to be reported in order to be effective. Its great advocate was Carmel Snow, who was one of the generation of female editors who, as she once said, wrote copy 'for well-dressed women with well-dressed minds' (cited in Rowlands, 2005, xiii). Irish-born, Snow was born into the midst of *La Belle Epoque*, in 1887. Textiles and fashion were in her genes, as her father, Peter White, worked for the Irish Woollen Manufacturing and Export Company, which worked to revive lace and other traditional crafts for a new era. As a child she would have gazed at the extraordinary lace dresses of Lady Aberdeen, as her father was made honorary secretary of the Irish Industries Association, of which she was patron. The family then moved to New York where Snow mixed with artists and the new band of 'lady decorators' emerging there. Edna Chase, the

formidable editor of *Vogue*, picked up Snow's ability in writing about the Paris collections that she had the privilege to attend, and she was made assistant fashion editor in 1921. The *Vogue* headquarters was subdued and elegant, with antique furnishings and a servants' zone. Condé Nast had purchased *Vogue* in 1909; it had been a society weekly in New York since 1892. It was selling about 16,000 copies by 1916, when British *Vogue* was inaugurated to deal with the

Figure 13 'Carmel Snow at work at Harper's Bazaar', contact sheet, photographer unknown, courtesy Diktats Bookstore.

blockades of war (Muir, 2002, p. 12). Condé Nast wanted his stable of magazines to reflect on fashions in all things as connected to contemporary writing and ideas (within limits), and therein lay its innovation. Snow shifted from writing to editing, noting of the practice, 'editors must be catalysts who communicate through their contributors' (Rowlands, 2005, p. 66).

Snow showed a profound interest in the fashion image, working all her career with innovative photographers who pioneered new techniques and approaches not just to models, but to 'inert' objects such as shoes and bags. Her involvement with Steichen was a true collaboration.

Like Diana Vreeland, Snow was something of a snob and believed in keeping up standards. The introduction of nail polish in the pages of the magazine in 1925 was sniffed at, and Snow reacted with horror to strapped shoes for day-wear as 'Inappropriate, unsightly, and dirty' (Rowlands, 2005, p. 82). But Snow was open-minded: 'The windows were always open, as if to everything new. Everything was so light, so sure, so concentrated' (quoted in Esten, 2001, p. 13). We see that clearly in Figure 13 in these contact sheets from around 1950, which show a modern woman, dressed in her Balenciaga uniform of a boxy suit, at work, editing. Carmel Snow retired in 1957.

Yves Saint Laurent – a 1970s analysis of 'The couturier and his brand'

Since the 1960s, youth fashions challenged the hierarchy of the fashion system. Fashion dictates were replaced with the notion of personal co-ordination of separates. People turned to second hand and old styles that had been old fashioned to make affronts to mass consumption, and the beatniks proposed a new style altogether. Many believed that the couture system might die, as the cult of youth accelerated. When Yves Saint Laurent used black in his early parade for Dior he was criticized for employing the colour of youthful protest and the bohemians of post-war Paris. For example, although the 82 year old Mrs T. Charlton Henry (Julia Rush Biddle) said 'I love the young', she added wistfully to an American newspaper journalist in 1968 that she could not possibly wear 'off the peg' clothes as she would end up looking like 'an old juvenile delinquent' (cited in Mayhew, n.d.).

The fashion boutique appeared for the first time, replacing the 'madame shops' or dress-makers that had once existed on street corners all around the western world. Young people had neither the money nor the snobbery to continue the ways of fashion that had dominated society until the Second World War. Whether this was a 'devaluation' of a great tradition or a cynical 'trickle down' is a matter of debate. One of the most cited theorists of fashion and proponent of a modified trickle-down theory is the sociologist Pierre Bourdieu, who used the society around him to generate a theory of culture in part based on his study of contemporary dressing.

In 1975 Bourdieu penned an account of the rise of the ready-to-wear *boutique*, which is associated most famously with Yves Saint Laurent and his 'Rive Gauche' (Left Bank) brand of 'off the peg'. In this important piece of writing composed with Yvette Delsaut, *Le Couturier et sa griffe: contribution à une théorie de la magique* (The couturier and his brand: contribution to a theory of magic) (Bourdieu and Delsaut, 1975), Bourdieu commenced with a quotation from the anthropologist Marcel Mauss concerning magic. Bourdieu then demystified the couture by exposing it as simply a field structured unequally between different 'houses' disposed within particular spaces of the city of Paris.

Bourdieu created his argument by analysing the spaces in which fashion is shown as much as the clothes themselves. Thus on one hand the white walls and grey wall-to-wall carpet of the grand Avenue Montaigne on the Right bank can be contrasted with the white and gold modern metal and volumetric forms that characterize the showrooms of the ready to wear on the Left Bank; a contrast between Louis Seize and Knoll furniture. Even the *vendeuses* are different; austere luxury and 'sober elegance' offered on the Right; the rather 'aggressive' and '*sainttropéziens*' (women who have summered in Saint Tropez) appearances of *des boutiques 'd'avant-garde'* of the Left (Bourdieu and Delsaut, 1975, p. 7).

Bourdieu argued that the devaluation entailed in 'mass appeal' of any product is most clearly visible in fashion, 'where the consecrated establishments are able to keep going for several generations' through exclusive concessions (Caron, Chanel) and other ageing hence 'vulgarised' brands (Coty, Worth) 'have a second career, down-market' (translated and cited in McNeil, 2011, p. 148). Bourdieu also explained the operation of designers not entitled by law to call themselves couturiers, the '*stylistes*' or '*modelistes*' who operated in the new era. 'Between the severe luxury of orthodoxy' of the consecrated houses, there was 'the ostensible ascetisicm of heresy', intensity of colours and even maybe trousers for women [author's translation] (Bourdieu and Delsaut, 1975, p. 8). It was precisely this type of designer who Yves Saint Laurent mocked in an interview made at this time. Asked whether he thought he was a great *couturier*, he noted, not yet, maybe in the future. Balenciaga and Miss Chanel are the greats, he stated. Then there are the show offs who use broken metal and funny parades to pretend they create design. And as for the majority of women, they are simply *bourgeoises* who wear a uniform of coiffed hair and pearls that Saint Laurent disparages as having nothing to do with fashion at all. On being asked how he would like to appear, he replied like a 'beatnik', but noted that he was now too old to ape the youth fashion style. He was being a tad ironic.

What is fashion irony? Mild sarcasm or feigning ignorance?

Perhaps we should start with the question 'does fashion irony exist?', but before we embark on debating its ontological status it might be useful to look at the concept of 'irony' and its emergence in Greek philosophy.

The dictionary definition of 'irony' is 'The humorous or mildly sarcastic use of words to imply the opposite of what they normally mean; an instance of this used to draw attention to some incongruity or irrationality, an incongruity between what is expected to be and what actually is, or situation or result showing such' (*Collins English Dictionary*, 2005, p. 856).

The word is derived from the Greek word *eironeia*, which translates as *dissimulation* or *feigned ignorance*, by extension also a rhetorical device used to great effect in philosophy as well as literature.

According to *Encyclopaedia Britannica*, its roots can be found in the Greek comic character Eiron, who constantly defeated with his clever bantering the foolish inanities of his opponent Algazon, and Socrates' own method, famously exemplified in Plato's early dialogue *Ion*, is the perfect demonstration. In it Socrates confronts the celebrated 'rhapsode' (professional reciter of the poetry of Homer) Ion from Ephesus with a dilemma: either he was totally ignorant or divinely inspired, a conclusion Socrates forced on Ion by using the humorous technique of feigned ignorance. One by one, Socrates demolished Ion's mistaken belief that he had true knowledge (*episteme*) about a number of professional skills such as that of the charioteer, the fisherman or the general, and forced him to accept his ignorance. In the end Ion accepted, gratefully at that, that he was no master of his subject, but divinely (as indeed Homer before him) inspired:

> Socrates But if you're not a master of your subject, if you're possessed by a divine gift from Homer, so that you make many lovely speeches about the poet without knowing anything – as I said about you – then you're not doing me wrong. So choose how do you want us to think of you – as a man who does wrong, or as someone divine?
> Ion There's a great difference, Socrates. It's much lovelier to be thought divine (Plato in Cooper, 1997, p. 949, 541e; 542b).

By extension 'irony' started being used as a rhetorical device, by predicating any number of artistic styles of it: classical, romantic, tragic, dramatic, verbal, poetic 'irony', and why not 'fashion irony'? But a distinction is immediately noticeable here: we do not have 'fashionable irony' that would provide the analogy with 'classical, romantic, etc.' irony; we have 'fashion irony'. In the case of the former, we have a perfect analogy with the definition of irony as feigned ignorance, in keeping with the Socratic example and examples abound.

But how does this work in fashion? How would we feign ignorance when faced with a humorous outfit by Viktor and Rolf, in order to imply the opposite of what they are visually showing? Hitherto 'irony' was used in literary criticism, but harder to apply to the visual arts where other adjectives are the preferred mode of approach of the critics. For that reason it may be useful to use an argument from analogy with the visual arts and it seems that in this context irony is conflated with other *genres* such as the cartoon, the caricature, political satire and so on, which are too 'in your face' to allow for the subtleties of ironic representations. An example springs to mind: the *Impossible Conversations* illustrated by the Mexican cartoonist Miguel Covarrubias and published in *Vanity Fair* in the 1930s. In it he paired the most improbable of celebrities: Sigmund Freud and Jean Harlow, Clark Gable and the Prince of Wales, and Stalin with Elsa Schiaparelli. And there is indeed splendid humour in the representations of Stalin and Schiaparelli dressed in green and bright red respectively hanging from parachutes (*Vogue*, June 1936) but they are not ironic; irony comes from their exchange of unpleasantries:

> STALIN You underestimate the serious goal of Soviet women.
> SCHIAPARELLI You underestimate their natural vanity.
> STALIN Perhaps I had better cut your parachute down!'
> SCHIAPARELLI 'A hundred other couturiers would replace me.
> STALIN In that case I better cut my own (Bolton and Harold, 2012, pp. 24–5).

Vanity Fair's 'Impossible Conversations' inspired an exhibition held at the Metropolitan Museum of New York, entitled *Schiaparelli and Prada: Impossible Conversations* (2012) curated by Harold Koda and Andrew Bolton. There is little doubt that the closest we can get to irony in fashion would be Elsa Schiaparelli, and her collaboration with the Surrealists is summed up as follows:

> Her surreal couture is both sinister and hilarious (Surrealism is a tragicomic genre) and it anticipates, by six decades, the mutant fantasies of Alexander McQueen and Martin Margiela. She designed a series of sublime cocktail hats in the shape of a lamb chop, high heels, and a vagina, and a pair of monkey-fur booties inspired by René Magritte (Thurman in Bolton and Harold, 2012, p. 28).

'Sublime cocktail hats in the shape of a lamb chop' provides a good example of the unspecific way in which criticism is applied in the fashion context because we are only beginning to see an incipient vocabulary of fashion criticism.

Where does that leave 'fashion irony?' If we turn to the internet we find 'ironic clothing' defined as: 'Wearing something unfashionable whilst seeming to attempt to be fashionable but both you and your audience need to be in on the joke. Our definition of irony involves taking something and making its wearing the direct opposite' (Shaw, n.d.).

We can think of one example which uncovers the genuine impossibility of applying irony in the proper sense of the definition to fashion: Miuccia Prada (in the catalogue of the exhibition mentioned above) stated, 'If I have done anything, it was making ugly cool' (Bolton and Harold, 2012, p. 26). One of the examples of 'ugly chic' by Prada in the exhibition is described as 'A three-piece Prada suit with a wraparound skirt, a boxy jacket, and a shapeless, high-necked top. The fabric is a stiff synthetic, digitally printed with a blurry grid. Each piece is a different awful colour (mustard, lime, mould green). It was modelled on the runway by Kate Moss, and even she couldn't pull it off' (Thurman in Bolton and Harold, 2012, p. 31).

In Umberto Eco's book *On Ugliness*, the history of ugliness is linked with morality (representations of the devil in religion) or humour (old age pretending to be otherwise), but none of these have equivalents in fashion, because Prada uses 'the ugly' as a lack, rather than an aesthetic category in its own right. The above outfit falls short of standards of *bon ton* and even 'Kate Moss' could not 'pull it off'. And who says that 'mustard, lime or mould green' need be ugly? . . . Could it not be suggested then that the only example which may approximate the use of irony in fashion comes from Lady Gaga and her meat dress?

Reporting on the Japanese revolution in Paris

When the Japanese fashion designers arrived in Paris, they created a veritable 'revolution' by the way they broke every rule in the book, not only regarding their clothes, but the way they were presented on the catwalk; by the models themselves, alien-looking and sombre; by the innovative materials they used, and what they did with them; but above all by the way they intertwined Japanese traditions with Western European *haute couture*. All of this resulted in a *Gesamtkunstwerk* of the kind not seen in Europe since the emergence of the Art Nouveau movement, in turn strongly influenced by late-nineteenth century *japonisme*. Japanese designers such as Rei Kawakubo (born 1942) for Comme des Garçons, Issey Miyake (born 1938) and Yohji Yamamoto (born 1943) rose to prominence in the 1970s. Without having any common programme, all have questioned eurocentric views of fashion and beauty. The Japanese reversed the western focus on symmetry and tidiness and adopted aspects of Japanese aesthetic systems such as the use by Yamamoto of black with colours such as red, purple, cerise, brown and dark blue.

The Japanese 'invasion' of Europe during the early 1980s, which constitutes the second wave of *japonisme*, has a precise point of inception: February 1982, when the then editor of the prestigious international art magazine *Artforum*, Ingrid Sischy, decided to use an outfit by Issey Miyake as its cover. The black outfit, which was a collaboration between Issey Miyake and the craftsman Koshige Shochikudo, who created the impressive rattan bodice recalling a samurai warrior's attire, was photographed for the magazine by Eiichiro Sakata. Sischy's radical gesture was not only perceived as a decisive moment which 'signalled the beginning of a new relationship between art and couture' (Wollen, 1998, p. 15) but it introduced at the same time a new approach to fashion through the contribution of the Japanese fashion designers and their links with the crafts: 'The Japanese designers, in particular – Issey Miyake, Rei Kawakubo at Comme des Garçons, Yohji Yamamoto – come from a tradition in which there is no clear-cut distinction between arts and crafts. Indeed, it is for this very reason that *japonisme* was such a major influence on the development of the original Arts and Crafts Movement in Europe' (Wollen, 1998, p. 16).

In 1854 Japan opened its gates for trade with Europe after a period of inaccessibility that goes back to 1638. The European market was subsequently 'flooded' with artefacts from Japan, specifically the arrival of the fabulous Japanese artists such as Katsushika Hokusai, Kitagawa Hiroshige and Utagawa Utamaro. Their prints had a far-reaching influence on the European visual arts starting with the Aesthetic movement and the *japonisme* of – among others – James Abbott McNeill Whistler, who 'from the early 1860s had begun to immerse himself in Oriental art and was trying to absorb it creatively into his own' (Honour and Fleming, 1982, p. 527). Whistler's radical stylistic vocabulary can be regarded as symptomatic of the impact of *japonisme* on the arts and crafts, very much in evidence in the first international European movement: Art Nouveau.

It was almost a century later that the second wave of *japonisme* arrived in Paris but on this occasion not in the arts, but in fashion, with its three seminal protagonists: Issey Miyake (born 1938), Rei Kawakubo (born 1942) and Yohji Yamamoto (born 1943). Their effect on the European fashion scene was perceived as:

A cleansing agent on the tastelessness and excesses of their British, American, French, and Italian counterparts. Their principles were asceticism and deconstructivism, with which they questioned every previously accepted norm. Japanese fashion was oversized and sacklike, consciously concealing the body instead of putting it centre stage. This was unique, new unheard of in the history of fashion. A fashion journalist consequently complained, 'Why should we pour all our money into health and fitness if we end up looking like tramps? (Schilling in Seeling, 2000, pp. 494–5).

To this journalist's comment, the redoubtable Suzy Menkes added her own after seeing a Comme des Garçons collection in Paris in 1983: 'My head feels drawn toward the Japanese . . . but the French can dress my body' (quoted in Seeling, 2000, p. 508).

In October 1982, Rei Kawakubo and Yohji Yamamoto held their second Paris fashion show, presenting a monochrome collection, mostly off-white outfits full of holes, shapeless and shabby, whose unexpected beauty evocative of transitoriness, the fragility of life and ultimately death, encapsulated the peculiarly Japanese *wabi sabi* aesthetics of imperfection. In an interview given to Susannah Frankel on the occasion of his first retrospective exhibition, entitled *Juste des Vêtements*, organized by the Musée de la mode et du textile in Paris, Yamamoto declared: 'I think perfection is ugly. Somewhere in the things humans make I want to see scars, failure, disorder, distortion. Perfection is a kind of order, like over all harmony and so on' (Frankel, 2005).

We saw him implementing his *wabi sabi* aesthetics in the asymmetric, distressed, mostly black garments, and more recently, at the exhibition organized at the Victoria and Albert Museum, London, dedicated to him in 2011.

Rei Kawakubo pushed the boundaries between the way the body and garments have been traditionally related to each other throughout the history of Western European costume, to an unacceptable extreme when she created in 1997 her collection of dresses with bumps, whose unique significance is beautifully summed up by Valerie Steele:

> Kawakubo not only challenges the social construction of woman as the beautiful sex, she also interrogates the entire idea of fashion. No longer is fashion a false surface that seeks to create the impression of a naturally beautiful female doll. Instead it exemplifies a new kind of embodiment. In her apparent pursuit of an alternative ideal of beauty, she denaturalizes all our assumption. The volume of dress may be compressed or stretched or otherwise distorted, as mutable forms imply impossible bodies. Comme des Garçons' famous *Dress becomes Body becomes Dress* collection of 1997, for example, was harshly criticized in the mainstream fashion press for 'deforming' the wearers (Steele and Park, 2008, pp. 69–73).

They recall the performance work of Louise Bourgeois (1911–2010) as well as the mannerism of eighteenth- and nineteenth-century underpinnings. Yohji Yamamoto also used the range of options of the western silhouette in reshaping dress. His ready-to-wear collection, launched in Paris in 1972, was entitled simply 'Y's', and was an affront to the *hauteur* of the Paris couture.

During the same year, while Kawakubo was fiendishly distorting the female body shape, Issey Miyake was experimenting with new ways of making clothes with the technique which came to be known as A-POC (acronym for 'a piece of cloth'), whereby in collaboration with the designer Dai Fujiwara they devised a new way of creating clothing by combining computer technology with traditional knitting methods, by creating free-sized garments that arrive as a knit tube. The wearer cuts out the desired clothing shapes from the tube, thus customizing the ready-made cloth (Nii in Fukai et al, 2002, p. 514).

But Miyake is best known for his wonderful 'pleats please', whereby he used pleating for a succession of seminal collections. In construing his clothes, however, Miyake changed the procedure, whereby instead of pleating the cloth first and then creating the outfit, he would start by creating it and then pleating the final result (Nii in Fukai et al, 2002, p. 514).

In this Issey Miyake shares the magical technique with the Italian designer Roberto Capucci (born 1930), whose 'sculpture dresses' have the eerie beauty of walking sculptures, something he does in fact share with Miyake's equally magical 'Flying Saucer' collection dated 1992, and so walking sculptures and walking lanterns, both beautifully pleated, go hand in hand.

There is no doubt that Capucci himself would have been influenced by Mariano Fortuny's use of pleating, but the question that remains to be asked is whether there is any link over and above the splendid sychronicity between Capucci and Miyake, a question that still remains to be answered. But for the time being Issey Miyake and Roberto Capucci created collections whose breathtaking beauty have effortlessly and genuinely made the art world their own.

Richard Martin as essayist: Karl Lagerfeld reworks Chanel

One of the great writers on fashion in the twentieth century who tended to write shorter rather than longer pieces is the late Richard (Harrison) Martin, who died from melanoma in 1999 at the age of 52. One of the most imaginative curators of fashion at the end of the twentieth century, Martin combined a keen sense of the materiality of dress with its intellectual history. His writing, in its sharp and sometimes arcane observation, recalled some of the fashion journalism of nineteenth-century Paris. He frequently referred to the relationship between art and fashion, without ever collapsing the two in a crude measure.

As well as being a superb curator, Martin was a brilliant essayist. He was a regular contributor to the newly established journal *Fashion Theory* led by the indomitable Dr Valerie Steele, who aimed to put the study of fashion on a serious critical level. To this end, she innovatively blended in her journal the full length refereed article of about 5,000–6,000 words, akin to an article in an art historical or historical journal, the gradual introduction of more regular book and exhibition reviews, the best of which did not simply report but rather tested the ideas expressed in a work, and also the 'essay' or note, in which shorter critical pieces on fashion were tested. The word essay come from the French 'to try' and that is all an essay is. It is one of the most important genres in academic writing, as much can be stated in an economical manner.

Richard Martin's essays on fashion are important contributions to fashion studies and their influence is probably under-estimated as he was not publishing the refereed articles and book-length monographs that reward academic life. Martin never argued that fashion was akin to art – in fact he opposed the idea – but he wished to see fashion as beyond the designerly or the commercial.

Martin was an art-history academic and a curator, first at the Fashion Institute of Technology and then at the Costume Institute at the Metropolitan Museum of Art, New York. Together with Harold Koda, he pioneered innovative ways of displaying fashion in the museum. One can never forget his exhibition *Gianni Versace* of 1997–98 at the Metropolitan Museum of Art, in which beaded garments were suspended above the viewers like the glittering mosaics of a Byzantine church. As this was the year of Versace's dreadful murder (1997), the exhibit had the added function of honouring a Catholic designer via other-worldly suggestions. Writing in *Fashion Theory* of the controversy that surrounded this exhibition – that it resembled the clothes of prostitutes and street walkers – Martin referred to the nineteenth-century strategy of elevating the 'carnal woman' that we discussed in Chapter 3, who, he writes, could be 'lifted by poetry into an acceptable empyrean' (Martin, 1998a, p. 96).

Let us now examine a few examples to see what he carried out. Richard Martin's work ranged very widely, and contained a strong gender, queer and political stance posited in a discreet but challenging manner at a time when such views were not widely expressed. Martin was fully expert in his field and aware of context and genre. Writing a discursive essay on the famous Versace 'safety pin' dress worn by the actress Liz Hurley, Martin argued that Versace, 'in this individual example and in the aggregate of this work, proves that contemporary fashion, empirically received by its immediate audiences, is also a cause for theory' (Martin, 1998a, p. 100). In his 'A Note, A Charismatic Art: The Balance of Ingratiation and Outrage in Contemporary Fashion', Martin described another Versace evening gown, this time made of PVC plastic (1995–96), in which Versace plays with the contrast between couture sewing and the visible machine stitching of jeans. Martin did this in order to illustrate his theory that fashion had a 'paradoxical intensity: we feel certain that we will be flattered or faked out, reinforced or rebuked, won over or run over' (Martin, 1997, p. 92). Fashion, to Martin, 'welcomes' and 'wheedles' and adds a 'rebarbative insult' (Martin, 1997, p. 92). In a world that thinks all fashion is just 'great' (consumption for dummies), what a welcome retort. Martin suggested some fashion contains a sting in its tail.

In an exquisite essay on a sailor's middy blouse, black leather, in spring–summer 1996 by Jean-Paul Gaultier, he noted that the garments from the wardrobes of humble occupations such as the sailor can be transformed in multiple ways, from the casual to the erotic: 'Gaultier works as a saboteur (who, after all, uses apparel as well) to disturb existing ideas and to offer the fashion object a new life' (Martin, 1997, p. 93). Without stating that Gaultier is an artist, Martin noted, 'Such a strategy would constitute a knowing simulation of the avant-garde and has been practiced at least since the 1960s by advanced visual artists in painting, sculpture, and cognate media' (Martin, 1997, p. 95).

Martin then concluded with an examination entitled 'Coromandel Charm', an indication that he understood his fashion and art history. Lagerfeld for Chanel fall–winter 1996 inverted Gabriel Chanel's modernity and encased his model in a lavishly embroidered extended cardigan or coat dress, a version of the coromandel screen, which decorated Chanel's apartment at the Ritz. The piece relates as well to the Chinese hybrid female garment, the *cheongsam*. In adopting the elements of venerated decorative arts, Lagerfeld's design elevates fashion, which so often is marginalized as trivial. As Richard Martin writes of this dress, Lagerfeld, like Gaultier, has an 'acute and buoyant knowledge of history, demanding that the past be assimilated into the present, but that the present can only tolerate and integrate a past that is specifically germane to modern living' (Martin, 1997, p. 95). Lagerfeld wraps the piece in an aura of art and power. Through such manoeuvres Lagerfeld proclaims his succession in the house of Chanel. And of course, the dress was photographed in Chanel's old stamping ground at the Ritz.

Being critical about 'deconstruction': theoretical approach or 'le destroy'?

In her essay entitled 'Deconstruction Fashion (The making of unfinished, decomposing and re-assembled clothes)', first published in *Fashion Theory* (1998), the Australian art and design historian Alison Gill starts by explaining the concept of 'deconstruction' within the fashion context, which – she observes – 'has entered the vocabulary of international fashion magazines, a label associated specifically with the work of Rei Kawakubo for Comme des Garçons, Karl Lagerfeld, Martin Margiela, Ann Demeulemeester and Dries Van Noten among others, and more loosely used to describe garments on a runway that are "unfinished", "coming apart", "recycled", "transparent" or "grunge"' (Gill in Barnard, 2007, p. 489).

The impressive number of uses of 'deconstruction' – which includes the styles encountered in the work of reputed fashion designers, as well as issues related to it such as ecology (recycling), movements (grunge), styles (unfinished) – notwithstanding, the polysemic definition of the term purloined from Jacques Derrida's philosophy testifies to its popularity: deconstruction itself became fashionable.

But why does fashion need philosophy in the first place? It is simple: as a new field of academic endeavour, 'fashion studies' which emerged in the 1980s, needed its own theoretical framework and so philosophy was regarded, alongside sociology, psychology, anthropology, ethnography and so on as a suitable candidate. Moreover, linked to another popular theoretical topic of the 1990s, 'is fashion art?', fashion turned to art for help.

When the *avant-garde* movements emerged at the beginning of the twentieth century, some of them (Cubism, Abstraction) were informed by theory, while others provided simply visually enjoyable aesthetic experiences (Fauvism). If we look at Cubism, Pablo Picasso's portraits from the 'analytic' period, such as that of his dealers Ambroise Vollard (1909) and Daniel-Henry Kahnweiler (1911) – where considerable skill is needed to discern the fellow's face amid all that faceting – cannot be said to provide an unmediated aesthetic pleasure, for it requires analysis. As a consequence, a vast literature emerged with for example the very use of the terms 'analytic' and 'synthetic', borrowed from the philosophy of Immanuel Kant.

As recently as 2001, the philosopher of science Arthur Miller published *Einstein, Picasso: Space, Time and the Beauty that Causes Havoc* (Basic Books, US), in which he argued that in *Les Demoiselles d'Avignon* (1907), Picasso was influenced by non-Euclidian geometry as well as writings on the fourth dimension postulated by the mathematician Henri Poincaré, who was a fashionable read among artists.

The same thing happened in the 1970s with linguistic philosophy, specifically the writings of Ludwig Wittgenstein (1889–1951), regarded as the greatest philosopher of the twentieth century, on this occasion resulting in work such as the conceptual group 'Art and Language'. Thus the now famous 'work of art' entitled *One and Three Chairs* (1965) by its founder Joseph Kosuth consisted of a 'real' chair, a photograph of a chair and the photography of the dictionary definition of a chair, juxtaposed together in an 'installation', which became the 'manifesto' for Kosuth's theories developed in his heavy hitting article 'Art after Philosophy', first published in *Studio International* (October 1969). Moreover, when Conceptual Art emerged in the early 1970s as an independent art movement, its aims and objectives were that 'conceptual artists take over the role of the critic in terms of framing their own propositions, ideas, and concepts' (Meyer, 1972, Introduction). Kosuth suggested that the reason was that 'the implied duality of perception and conception in earlier art, a middleman (critic) appeared useful. This (conceptual) art both annexes the functions of the critic and makes the middleman unnecessary' (Kosuth in Meyer, 1972, Introduction). Like analytical propositions in philosophy (mathematics) which are self-referential and tautological, Kosuth argued, so too is conceptual art, and so the three chairs are a perfect example of a massive tautology. Artistic value? Non-existent.

Wittgenstein provided the concept of 'family resemblance' usable in examples such as 'art', which does not have a logical definition in terms of necessary and sufficient conditions; instead it could be defined in terms of 'family resemblance', rather like 'games'. Wittgenstein's examples are linked to each other in a kind of criss-crossing, which have similarities and dissimilarities between them, but belong to the same logical category.

We find 'family resemblance' also used in fashion by a theorist with a background in philosophy: in his book *Fashion as Communication* (2002) Malcolm Barnard compares the definition of fashion which incorporates a wealth of other words, 'dress', 'attire', 'costume' and so on, as related in a criss-crossing way, linked by their 'family resemblance', as proposed by Wittgenstein, but in this instance, Barnard's use of Wittgenstein is relegated to semantics, while Gill uses 'deconstruction' for clothes.

Jacques Derrida (1930–2004) – rather like Martin Heidegger and Ludwig Wittgenstein before him – is an 'anti-philosopher', who aimed at nothing less than to re-write Western European philosophy, by 'deconstructing' it. The term was borrowed from phenomenology and the writings of Edmund Husserl and Martin Heidegger who used it for 'destroying the history of ontology', but *destruktion* did not mean destruction, rather a 'de-structuring', or as Derrida would have it, 'deconstructing', whereby instead of destroying traditional philosophy, Heidegger set out on the task of 'retrieving it as a philosophy to come – a future philosophy that will look forward to its past and revel in its endless novelty' (Rée in Monk and Raphael, 2001, p. 362).

In his own analysis of text (like Heidegger before him, Derrida, too, set out to re-write Western European philosophy). He employed the term 'deconstruction' to uncover 'imaginative exposures of gaps, transgressive possibilities, or unintended indicators', all of which lead to 'a multiplicity of readings' (Appleby et al, 1996, p. 18).

While Derrida's writings belong to philosophy, his new analytical tool, deconstruction, became very popular in other disciplines, notably literature, and in the writing of critics such as Paul de Man, whose interest focused on the conflict between logical writing and figural language so that meaning needs to be uncovered through deconstruction. That becomes the responsibility of the astute critic to elucidate (Norcross in Payne, 1997, p. 138).

Gill quotes Mary McLeod, who argued that the exhibition 'Deconstructivist Architecture' held at MOMA, New York, in 1988 popularized the label with examples of work such as that of Peter Eisenman, who collaborated with his friend, Derrida. The question is, can architecture be viewed as a visual language and subjected to deconstructive analysis just like a literary or philosophical text? Not everybody agrees: the architectural historian Kenneth Frampton, for instance, regards deconstruction in architecture as 'elitist and detached'.

Alison Gill applies 'deconstruction' without further ado to the work of Martin Margiela who, by turning the garment inside out, was supposed to uncover the process of making, but its true justification – according to Gill – is that we can regard deconstruction in fashion as: 'something like an auto-critique of the fashion system: It displays an almost X-ray capability to reveal the enabling conditions of fashion's bewitching charms (i.e. charms conveyed in the concepts ornament, glamour, spectacle, illusion, fantasy, creativity, innovation, exclusivity, luxury repeatedly associated with fashion) and the principles of its practice (i.e. from, material, construction, fabrication, pattern, stitching, finish)' (Gill in Barnard, 2007, p. 491)

The French even came up with '*le destroy*', conceivably a Gaelic-free translation of the heavier German '*Destruktion*', in turn Anglicized into 'deconstruction', but '*le destroy*' acquires an additional dimension in addition to Margiela's processes, to do with punk sensibilities, grunge, piercing, slashing and other destructive aspects identifiable either in the subcultural or mainstream fashion contexts.

The question that needs to be posed at the end of all this is: 'What is it in aid of?' For Derrida, 'deconstruction' is a tool for critical analysis confined to the arcane context of academe from where it sprang, via the Phenomenologists. In architecture (as a privileged form of visual art) deconstruction was proposed as a new stylistic language often employed in specific examples: Daniel Liebeskind's Jewish Museum in Berlin built as a locus of memory.

But why 'deconstruction' in fashion? Perhaps the ironic dimension invoked above may well point us to Marx's 'fetishism of the commodities' or to some such form of ideological criticism against fashion regarded as a frivolous luxury commodity, but in the end, the punters will not buy a 'falling apart' (deconstructed) garment to wear, unless on its back we have the mysterious blank white label which is no longer that mysterious, for everybody knows that it is the 'deconstructed' signature of Martin Margiela, who never appears in public or allows himself to be photographed, but whose name alone brings in business.

What is a reviewer?

Confusing as this may appear *prima facie*, the reviewer is the critic! The 'new' term was coined-up in journalism for some obscure reason very likely to do with the perceived 'high-brow' content inherent in all the issues to do with critics, criticism and what is criticized (allegedly relegated also to the 'high-brow' arts), while the term 'reviewer' appears more user-friendly, democratic and therefore accessible to all.

For that reason we will replace the question of 'what is a reviewer' with that of 'what is a critic' and we start from the beginning by providing a dictionary definition of criticism, which is as good as any starting point, and from which we singled out the first three definitions taken from *Collins English Dictionary*:

- the act of an instance of making an unfavourable or severe judgement, comment, etc.
- the analysis or evaluation of a work of art literature, etc.
- the occupation of a critic.

Thus criticism is what critics do and what critics do is to evaluate (for example make a value judgement: this is good, not so good, bad or really bad) about X, where X can be a painting, a film, a book, a play, a photograph, a building or a piece of music. To this traditional list of what is generally accepted as belonging to the pantheon of the sister arts – painting, sculpture and architecture – two relative newcomers were added (from the second half of the nineteenth century) – photography and film – whose status as art or mechanical forms of reproducing reality continues to be debated, although certain types of film and certain types of photography are easily accepted as art today. An even newer candidate to be included is fashion. As with photography and the cinema before, the question to ask is whether fashion is art and if so can we identify an aesthetics of fashion by establishing a specificity of 'the fashion element' – perhaps a neologism would be in order here – such as (fashionabilical), analogous to the 'photographic' in a photograph, or the 'filmic' in a film, to enable us to outline that unique dimension pertaining to fashion? The following brief survey of the emergence of an incipient vocabulary of and for fashion criticism reveals some interesting conclusions.

In the case when we deal with a functional object we call craft, nobody in their right mind would bother to ask whether a piece of furniture or a spoon resolutely pertaining to the crafts is art, because the final cause for which they were created was functionality. Nevertheless it seems acceptable to admire a Chippendale chair or an Alessi spoon for criteria such as harmony of proportions, details of decoration, colour and so on, which have nothing to do with how well they fulfil their functions *qua* objects to sit on or eat with.

The functional aspect of our clothes is still considered the main obstacle in considering fashion as art, but however visually seductive they are, art it aint't for the obvious reason: we wear them. But how about architecture? After all, however perfect a building such as the Parthenon is, its architects meant it for a functional purpose, and yet nobody will dispute its artistic merits or its status established during the Quattrocento by the Aristotelian humanist Lorenzo Valla, who was the first to classify painting, sculpture and architecture as the 'fine arts'.

Confirmation about the artistic status of fashion comes from the reputable pen of Anne Hollander: in *Seeing Through Clothes* she states categorically that 'dress is a form of visual art, a creation of images with the visible self as its medium' (1993, p. 311). If we accept Hollander's definition as the premise for the argument, we can proceed by postulating a critical vocabulary of fashion and the starting point comes from none other than Charles Baudelaire (1821–67), whom as we have already read, in his *salon* review of the graphic work of Constantin Guys, better known under the title 'The Painter of Modern Life' (1863), made a bold statement about fashion: 'All fashions are *charming* or rather relatively *charming*' (Baudelaire, 1972, pp. 465–7).

Not only as a pioneering fashion critic but one of the first professional critics of the *salons*, Baudelaire needed an authoritative vocabulary, and for fashion he chose the adjective 'charm', which he purloined from his own literary writings, as the following poem entitled 'For a Creole Lady' from his *Fleurs du mal* demonstrates: 'A place where indolence drops on the eyes like rain/I met a creole lady of unstudied grace'. It is interesting that in the French original we have: '*une dame créole aux charmes ignorés*' (Baudelaire, 1993, pp. 128–9) whereby the translator replaced 'charm' with 'grace'. The relevant issue, however, is Baudelaire's choice of the word 'charm', which he predicated of fashion.

It worked, because we find it used in the pioneering reviews written about fashion in fashion magazines during their heyday period between the last decades of the nineteenth century and the first two of the twentieth century. They reveal that alongside a number of innocuous terms such as '*folie*', '*elegant*' and '*delicieux*', both 'charm' and 'grace' were used regularly, signalling an incipient critical vocabulary for fashion writing.

One such example comes from Martine Rénier's column for the magazine *Les Élégances parisiennes* (October 1916), in which she reviews the collections of Jeanne Lanvin, whose outfits she declared to be '*éclatante*' (stunning) and '*delicieux*' (delicious); then Worth, Chéruit and Paquin: '*nous montre toute une serie de petites robes simples et très élégantes*' (we show a series of little, simple and very elegant dresses) whose detailing of small pockets and amusing embroidery gave them '*un charmant cachet*' (a charming cachet).

In the November 1916 issue we find a reviews of new designs by Jenny, Martial, Armand and Beer: '*Dans la jolie collection très parisienne de Beer je distingue quelques mélanges de tous et d'étoffes absolument charmants*' (in the pretty and very Parisian collection by Beer I distinguish some mixtures of 'stuffs' [materials] that are absolutely charming). Thus we can single out in this example of critical writing a staple diet including: '*charmant*' (charming), '*éclatant*' (striking), '*élégant*' (elegant) and '*delicieux*' (delicious).

If we move fast-forward to the 1940s, no change regarding the critical terminology used by fashion writers is visible, or indeed regarding the balance of power: Worth, Lanvin, Patou, Lelong still dominated the Parisian fashion world. There were, however, two notable newcomers 'on the block': Cristóbal Balenciaga and Elsa Schiaparelli. It was their unorthodox approach that found favour with the anonymous reviewer of *L'Officiel et de la couture et de la mode de Paris*, who used new words to express their originality. In the March 1940 issue, the reviewer emphasized their courage to deviate from the canonical mainstream style: '*Il y a tant de jeunnesse et de caractère dans les modèles de Printemps préséntés par Schiaparelli que l'on sent que leur créatrice dut prendre plaisir à les composer*' (There is so much youthfulness and character in the Spring models presented by Schiaparelli that one feels that their creator took great pleasure in creating them) (*L'Officiel de la couture*, 1940). Balenciaga too is praised for originality: '*L'originalité profonde de le créateur s'impose des le premier modèle de sa nouvelle collection*' (The profound originality of the creator impresses itself from the first model of his new collection). '*Originalité profonde*' (profound originality) and '*jeunnesse*' (youthfulness) are two good terms employed by the writer. Mainstream *couturiers*, however, were still evaluated by using the 'old' vocabulary, for example '*grace delicate*' (delicate grace) or '*amusant*' (amusing). Thus in an entry about one of the 'sacred cows' of the establishment, Jeanne Paquin, we find: '*La variété des robes d'aprés midi est infinie et les details de leurs garnitures sont d'une grace delicate. Un modèle de la campagne comprend un amusant effet de culottes à petits volants*' (The variety of afternoon dresses is infinite and the details of their trimmings are of a delicate grace. A countryside model comprises an amusing effect with culottes with little skirts).

A survey of contemporary fashion writing reveals some interesting developments and although it would be facile to draw a definitive conclusion from such a scant survey, an example from the *Financial Times* (25–26 May 2013), chosen as a case study here, reveals that the emphasis switched from concepts used in an evaluative sense, whether borrowed from the arts, such as 'charm', or created for fashion – 'elegant' and 'glamorous' – to a descriptive terminology which complies with Roland Barthes' 'written text', first written in 1967 and reproduced in *The Language of Fashion* (Barthes, 1990), in which he privileged the above 'image text' as the more popular for the format of the fashion magazine, and clearly that can be extended to newspaper fashion writing. In an article entitled 'It's Tea Dress Time' Melanie Abrams exalts the merits of the 1940s tea gown, which made a comeback: 'Take for example, Bottega Veneta's floral version spotted with studs; Valentino's snakeskin and lace combos; or Loewe's tough leather looks. Then there is Etro's blue style with sexy cut-out back (£810) and Balenciaga's understated white poplin mini (£865)' (Abrams, 2013).

Like her predecessors, Abrams reviews the collections of the great and the good, but no terms such as 'elegant', 'charming', 'graceful' are in sight; instead the focus is on materials: snakeskin, leather; a bit more poetic though, with regard to Etro's 'blueness', and an evaluative concept is also allowed for none other than Balenciaga: 'understated'!

Like criticism itself, this text is best left open-ended as we cannot offer a conclusion, although it is possible to comment that fashion writing has produced its own history.

What gives Suzy Menkes the status of professional critic?

The answer is, nothing at all! She had to acquire, create and deserve it! We could – playfully perhaps – paraphrase William Shakespeare's immortal ruminations about greatness from the play *Twelfth Night, or What you Will*: 'Some are born great, some achieved greatness and some have greatness thrust upon 'em' (Shakespeare, 1980, p. 332) by replacing 'greatness' with 'the professional critic'.

Thus, to even state that a professional critic can be born is an oxymoron; professionalism or professional status is seldom thrust on the lucky critic, but if possible, however improbable, the only way then to gain such an elevated status (greatness) – and nobody would dispute Suzy Menkes's right to it – is to achieve it! This is all very well, but the really interesting issue is how to go about it.

Suzy Menkes (born 1943) studied history and English literature at Newnham College, Cambridge University, and she started her writing career by publishing books on topics from Royal jewels to the lifestyle of the Duke and Duchess of Windsor and working as a fashion reporter for *The Times*. In 1988 she became style editor at the *International Herald Tribune* and that more or less set her on her path to achieving recognition as one of the most respected professional critics in the fashion world.

Now fashion criticism itself may itself still be regarded as an oxymoron: criticism is something that we apply to the arts, while fashion is resolutely located in the world of big money spinning, success, glamour, power and so on . . . nothing to wax lyrical about for the critic, much to be cynical about instead!

Nevertheless, the subject of this very book is not only to analyse the origins and historical development of criticism, but also to argue that fashion has been queuing patiently in line to acquire a critical vocabulary of its own. Like the history of art before it, which lacking a critical vocabulary, simply purloined it from other disciplines – literary criticism, literature, history and so on – so too fashion – being regarded as part and parcel of the visual arts – followed suit, and we find Charles Baudelaire borrowing the adjective 'charming' – a great favourite in his own poetry – and predicating it of fashion!

Criticizing the critics involves using a meta-language and that would be quite a challenge, as fashion criticism is still struggling to become established practice; instead we propose an analytical survey of some of Suzy Menkes's articles in order to see how she uses her knowledge, craft and specialized vocabulary to achieve the results which attracted such an accolade for her writing in the first place. The following three examples come from *The New York Times*.

The first example is 'Red Carpet Baggers (Women's Fashion)', published on 14 February 2012. Menkes uses irony to make an interesting point, which can be used as an analogy for establishing a critic's credentials: she asks whether 'anybody can be a designer', which – as she observes – is now 'part of the culture. Celebrities, stylists and enthusiasts on "Project Runway" are all aiming to join Karl & Co'. She subsequently provides an outline of how this situation became implemented, using a wealth of examples that reveal her in-depth knowledge regarding the 'behind-the-scene' goings-on of the fashion world. She enumerates celebrity endorsements, for example Jennifer Lopez, Gwen Stefani and Elizabeth Taylor; the rise of the celebrity magazines throughout the 1990s; and celebrities turned fashion designers, starting with Victoria Beckham supported by her footballer husband David Beckham, followed by other famous partnerships such as L'Wren Scott and Mick Jagger, and of course Lady Gaga and her stylist Nicola Formichetti, who was instrumental in launching her as the most notorious international star on the circuit: 'not only can Formichetti take some credit for the infamous red meat dress, he's also reviving the Thierry Mugler label with a runway assist from Lady Gaga'.

Indeed, if we 'Google' Lady Gaga, Wikipedia introduces her as: 'an American singer-songwriter, record producer, activist businesswoman, fashion designer and actress'. Had she chosen to be introduced as 'a brain surgeon, tree surgeon, chiropodist, train driver and gardener' there might have been some raised eyebrows, but nobody seems to bat an eyelid regarding her enviable list of professional skills; in fact her credentials are accepted and even Menkes herself nods approval, albeit indirectly.

The moot question Menkes asked herself as fashion editor is 'whether taste and style are really a match for creativity and experience?' but she does not answer, apart from making a discreet confession: 'I get mad thinking how tough it is for talented young "creatives" to get financing while stars are lavished because they're already famous'. Indeed, she depicts a loopy world if ever there was one, and even if we accept that the celebrity cult is not new (consider Coco Chanel, Jacqueline de Ribes, Diane von Furstenberg or Carolina Herrera), nevertheless there is iniquity in the *status quo*. Menkes herself appears to sit on the fence, but she regales us with a splendidly ironic closing paragraph and example, and leaves us (cleverly) to interpret it as we will. She asks: 'What do "real" designers think of their celeb competitors? Mostly they say, "don't give up the day job". Alber Elbaz, who, by way of Israeli design school, an apprenticeship at Geoffrey Beene and a stint at Saint Laurent, repositioned Lanvin as a red-hot brand, put his reaction to pop stars-turned-style gurus like this: "And maybe I should sing?" '

The second example is 'Cabinet of Curiosities (Fashion Review)', published on 4 July 2013. This is a fine example of Suzy Menkes in action as fashion critic, evaluating the collections presented in Paris for autumn 2013. Among them, she selected several collections starting with the Dutch duo Viktor and Rolf, which she sums up succinctly: 'The Viktor and Rolf collection, with its sculptural shapes and Zen spirit, also was beautiful in its ascetic way, going deeply into the conceptual realm, with no idea that could be defined as seasonal clothing.' The emphasis is on asceticism, spirituality and universality, but the key point is that the beauty of their collection is a conceptualist approach that transcends the particular and strives towards acquiring a universal dimension. How lovely is this!

For Valentino, his followers who now create the Collection, Maria Grazia Chiuri and Pierpaolo Piccioli, turned to cabinets of curiosities for inspiration and even included them in their display. The review concludes with another 'classical' *maison de couture* who – like Valentino – continues its existence under a different leadership, namely Vionnet, at present owned by Goga Ashkenazi, who is also chief executive and designer and who, Menkes commented, 'is trying to restore the Vionnet style and spirit'. Is it possible, and if so, does it also work? We may well ask, and we may well even question the ethical aspect (as pointed elsewhere in this volume) of such current practices. However, we are not told by Suzy Menkes, who diplomatically avoided to offer her views; instead she concludes her review with a delicate but telling comment: 'But haute couture is a craft as well as an art. And maybe for all her enthusiasm, this designer/owner should set up a studio of "little hands" to make the Vionnet clothes as beautiful in execution as in the original thought.'

The third example is 'The Colourful History of the Little Black Dress' (exhibition at the Mona Bismarck American Center for Art and Culture, Paris), published on 5 August 2013. The exhibition created by Savannah College of Art and Design (SCAD) in Georgia and curated by André Leon Talley – contributing editor of *American Vogue* and now an editor at large for the Russian version of *Numeró* magazine – is introduced by Menkes as follows: 'The exhibition pits a framed Karl Lagerfeld example of the classic black Chanel dress, as worn by Anna Wintour, the editor-in-chief of *American Vogue*, against the feisty cutaway Latex dress by Norma Kamali, or even a body-revealing lace and jet-beading creation from Tom Ford.'

But Leon Talley also has high connections and that is a credential which more than qualifies him for the job, for not only did he 'enrich the collection that opened in 2011 at the SCAD Museum of Art in Savananah', but more importantly his experience derives from: 'years of attending haute couture shows and advising socialites like Anne Bass, a benefactor of the New York City Ballet, as well as famous names from Alicia Keys through Gwyneth Paltrow, Diana Ross, Serena and Venus Williams and Renée Zellweger'. A refreshing list, which reveals Talley to be entrenched not in the world of money, but culture, the arts and sport, which is not about money or social status; rather it privileges a meritocracy which renders it more democratic, although money is useful.

The exhibition starts with Mona Bismarck herself, the first woman in the world to head a 'best dressed' list in 1933, and that is the reason why it was organized at her former home in Paris, at present 'The Mona Bismarck American Center for Art and Culture'. But then the displays move away from classical elegance to incorporate 'hyper-modern dresses' where Menkes uses Barthes's 'written image' approach, starting with the American designer Prabal Gurung's 'plunge-front gown, Diane Von Furstenburg's synthetic *lamé* wrap dress and a Neoprene zip-front design from the SCAD graduate Alexis Asplundh'.

Finally the real aims and objectives of this exhibition are summed up as follows: 'So is the little black dress the last haven for a conventional dresser, or an opportunity to add a jolt of imagination to a classic?' The conclusion is both of course, and Miuccia Prada is quoted to sum it all up: 'Miuccia Prada expresses the reality of timeless yet contemporary fashion, when she says in the book: "To me, designing a little black dress is trying to express in a simple, banal object, a great complexity about women, aesthetics, and current times." '

Acne Paper: the beauty of print, the splendour of the page

Acne Paper has a cult following, an indication that beauty will always win out over banality. *Acne Paper* is the brainchild of a Swedish fashion company, Acne Studios, headed by the urbane Mikael Schiller as CEO and now chairman, who is also its publisher. Acne's mid-priced clothing stores are immediately recognizable around the world for their eye-popping accessories and chic minimalist interiors. The Stockholm flagship store is in fact in the space of the former banking building whence the name 'Stockholm syndrome' developed. *Acne Paper* was a collaboration 'between Acne, Acne Art Dept, Acne Film, Acne JR, Acne Digital, and Acne Creative' (*Acne Paper*, 2008, p. 162). It is now solely published by Acne Studio and is therefore unlike most other fashion magazines as it is a marketing tool for one fashion brand, even though other brands (generally Japanese or other 'directional' ones) are shown in its fashion spreads.

Acne Paper is a large format broadsheet that is retailed in the better class of newsagencies around the world and also available via subscription across the internet. Clearly not a money making endeavour (in 2009 one year's subscription was €19), the publication adds value to a brand. It is possibly modelled on the format of a 1970s Swedish photographic magazine, *Papper* (1984–2001), which had a similar large format and covered art, culture and life. *Papper* was free, exclusive and luxurious, and was sponsored by Lars Hall, a prominent collector, dealer and gallerist (Galleri Camera Obscura, Stockholm, which might have been the first to show fashion photography as art in Sweden). The title was also a pun on the huge Swedish forestry and paper industry.[2]

Many people tend to see *Acne Paper* following on from Andy Warhol's magazine *Interview*, as the interview and large format is its calling card, creating an immediacy and freshness and removing the magazine from the sense of 'advertorial' copy. *Acne Paper* takes very little advertising, generally something discreetly inserted in one section for a high quality product such as 'Standard Hotels'. Thomas Persson, its editor in chief and creative director, takes a cue from the large format and double bleed promoted by Diana Vreeland in the 1950s and 1960s, developing a theme for each issue, commissioning articles and photography. The paper is specially sourced and the quality of the matte printing, layout and typography exceptionally high, the print conducted at Rotolito Lombarda, Italy. Central to the success of the periodical is the fashion director Mattias Karlsson with whom Persson has collaborated from the beginning. Editor at large is Jonny Johansson, creative director of Acne Studios and a well-known figure in fashion and design circles in Sweden. Editors have included Anja Aronowsky Cronberg (who now edits from Paris the innovative advertisement-free fashion periodical *Vestoj*) and Charlotte Rey.

A part of the power of the magazine revolves around its knowing and sometimes surprising juxtapositions. Let us consider one issue, Summer 2008. Its theme was 'Exoticism'. Yet the first nine pages depicted some 1960s North American nuns conducting an art class and a series of inverted *papiers collés* that looked like outsider art. These were identified in captions at the back of the magazine as 'Sister Corita' at work, who created serigraphs at what is now the Corita Art Center, Immaculate Heart Community, Los Angeles, and they indeed date from 1962 to 1967. The serigraphs are given their media and dimensions and dates, and thus retain their dignity as art works, rather than simply being decontextualized in a post-modern 'grab'. The nun's habits make a wonderful foil to the bright coloured shirts of the 1960s gentleman and young lady who are shown working with them in the art workshop. The cover image, a photograph by Terry Tsiolis, was styled by Mattias Karlsson and depicted the model Jonté wearing a dress by Comme des Garçons. Unnatural coloured green and purple pigment was blended across the androgynous face and neck of the model of colour, who also sports a top-knot of green dyed hair, recalling some of Vreeland's fun with 'Dynel' in the 1960s. He was shot in profile. The image therefore recalled both anthropological photography of the nineteenth century and the hauteur of the inter-war fashion photograph.

What are the contents of this magazine? Models of colour shot in balletic movement wearing Japanese designer fashion and revealing much of their bodies. Clothes worn unconventionally, a purple satin skirt as a turban, for instance, but shot in black and white and therefore not easily recognisable. Christopher Breward, the well-known fashion historian and theorist, was interviewed by Helen Mears, African Disapora Research Fellow at the Victoria and Albert Museum, about exoticism in the eighteenth century. One would not expect a diaspora specialist to be interviewed in a fashion magazine. The story was illustrated with a full-page image from Hogarth, also not what one expects in a contemporary fashion magazine. The musical scores of Howard Shore were analysed via an interview; the inspiration of the stylist Nicola Formichetti analysed

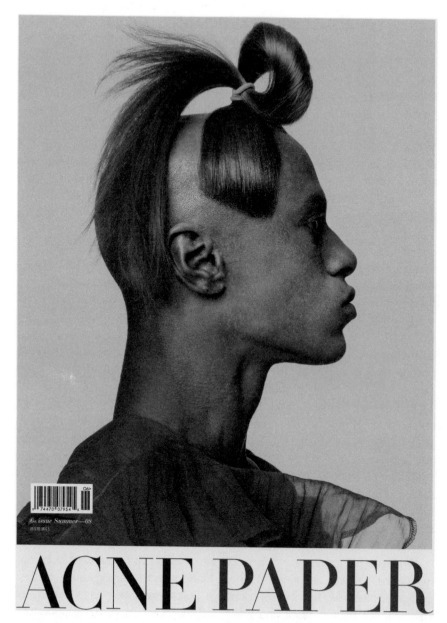

Figure 14 Cover, *Acne Paper*, 6th issue, Summer 2008, photograph by Terry Tsiolis, styling Mattias Karlsson, the model Jonté wearing a dress by Comme des Garçons, with permission and copyright *Acne Paper*.

through an edited first person narrative; the Director of Mariage Frères' exquisite teas interviewed about the history and qualities of great tea, once again illustrated with a beautiful eighteenth-century engraving of 'the tea tree'. Nancy Ireson, a museum curator, was interviewed about the primitivist painter Henri Rousseau; and so it goes on. Exquisite and surprising stories about art, culture and design were interspersed with essays, works of art by figures as important as Robert Mapplethorpe and Horst P. Horst; and a queer element introduced via an interview with the drag troupe 'The Cockettes'. Superb double page images of Rolf de Maré and the Ballets Suédois were complemented by an intelligent interview with a dance curator, Erik Näslund.

What to conclude about this artefact? Is it a fashion magazine at all? – its very name *Acne Paper* is deliberately ambiguous. This answer is yes, it is a fashion magazine, but one that calls to attention the art and artifice that goes into the fashion industry. Its very large A3 size and extremely heavy paper makes the reader slow down and reflect somewhat differently. The artefact does not feel disposable. Through its clever editorial decisions, large budget and high production values, it gives a dignity to the photographers, designers, stylists, writers and even humble academics who engage with fashion, which sets it apart from most other such periodicals today. Now much copied in size and format around the world, it is yet to be exceeded in beauty and thoughtfulness.

How to be a 'critical' blogger: moving beyond the PR release

How was it with Andy Warhol's '15 minutes of fame' when he predicted that 'in the future everyone will be world-famous for 15 minutes'? The year was 1968.

Since those heroic times when Marshall McLuhan was waxing lyrical about the 'global village', Andy Warhol's '15 minutes of fame' penetrated the collective consciousness and became a much used expression, to the extent of being used indiscriminately, even if most people don't even know its origin. Not that it matters anyway, but we are of the firm opinion that Andy Warhol's prediction be adopted as the bloggers' motto, because they made it come true.

What is 'blogging' anyway and where does it come from? Wikipedia (we might as well simply turn to the net as many bloggers do) tells us that the word 'blog' was coined in the late 1990s. Like Wikipedia itself – which among its multiple uses is a wonderful basic tool for the researcher (we know you all use it) – blogging is entrenched in the brave new world of information technology: in the 1990s the invention of the world wide web was coined by Tim Berners-Lee and blogging itself emerged as an exercise in keeping an online diary. Blogging is generally accepted to have been launched in 1994 with Justin Hall telling the world about himself.

It becomes immediately obvious why 'blogging' is such a marvellous tool for those passionate about fashion, for what can be more exciting than creating a 'fashion diary', and this is exactly what happened; they swiftly become 'a significant space of identity construction' (Rocamora, 2011, p. 407). One example, more connected with the beauty and fragility of youth, is Thi Nguyen's *Chasing Strangers*, whose manifesto states: 'SKIN recognises the power of words to amplify the power of pictures: SKIN inherits the legacy of Andy Warhol, Rennie Ellis and German New Objectivity. Conceived in 2009, SKIN is the first methodical and pro bono attempt to enshrine everyday dwellers of the metropolis in Australia and across the globe. Get in touch and get involved.' The portraits refer both to the rise of the individuated portrait in fifteenth-century Italy as well as the contemporary urban street; Nguyen is, in fact, currently a university student of art history, and his blog shows wit and erudition.

By now the world is filled with very famous fashion bloggers in search of 15 minutes of global fame but it would be fair to say that the wonder child of fashion blogging is Tavi Gevinson; she certainly transcended the 15 minute limit and inserted herself in the short history of blogging as a pioneer. In fact Lady Gaga proclaimed 'blogging' to be the future of journalism, in which case it would be more fruitful to look forward rather than to assess historically Tavi Gevinson's achievements during the short span of her career, which started when she was twelve years old. Suffice it to say that at age eleven she capitalized on the availability of social networks to create in 2008 her own fashion blog 'Style Rookie', which brought her the fame she might or might not have courted with invitations to the New York and Paris fashion weeks, interviews in the top newspapers and magazines, and modelling for *Rodarte*. But in 2011 she decided to redesign her blog into a more inclusive publication: and so *Rookie Magazine* was founded. Wikipedia introduces her as an American writer, magazine editor, actress and singer, and no doubt the list will continue to grow, though it is difficult to predict in which direction. One thing is certain, the genius of this young blogger consisted in being able to capitalize on the splendid opportunities on offer which she put to good use from the comfort of her own home, room and computer but above all, Tavi Gevinson addressed an even younger 'teen' generation – very different in aims and objectives from the American youth culture of the 1950s when the concept of the 'teen' emerged to designate a new class of consumers, the teenagers – her own.

Agnès Rocamora has recently painted a precise picture of the challenge of understanding the fashion blog. Critiques of blogs, she notes, can be 'seen in the light of what some have argued is a crisis of the 'expert paradigm' (Rocamora, 2013, p. 159). Furthermore, she reminds us, again via the writing of Marshall McLuhan, that 'new media may well transform established visions, but they never totally supersede old media, for a new medium always appropriates some of the characteristics of an older medium' (Rocamora, 2013, p. 160).

Figure 15 'Alex Gibson-Giorgio', photographed 20 February 2013, from Thi Nguyen's website chasingstrangers.com, Thi Nguyen, SKIN | Creative Direction, Australia; facebook.com/skinarchive, with permission from Thi Nguyen, trong.au@gmail.com

How then does 'blogging' work as the 'new' criticism? We selected Suzy Menkes's article 'The Circus of Fashion' published in Tmagazine.blogs.nytimes. com) on 10 February 2013, which attracted 79 comments from bloggers, ranging from the sycophantic to the disapproving. As the title suggests, she considered exactly the kind of public events, call them spectacles if you will, created very intentionally by the fashion world, such as fashion weeks organized in the major capitals of Europe and the USA, whose sarcastic opening paragraph informs the reader what the article is about:

> We were once described as 'black crows' – us fashion folk gathered outside an abandoned, crumbling downtown building in a uniform of Comme des Garçons or Yohji Yamamoto. 'Whose funeral is it?' passers-by would whisper with a mix of hushed caring and ghoulish inquiry, as we lined up for the hip, underground presentations back in the 1990s. Today, the people outside fashion shows are more like peacocks than crows. They pose and preen, in their multi-patterned dresses, spidery legs balanced on club-sandwich platform shoes, or in thigh-high boots under sculptured coats blooming with flowers.

Menkes is arguing that the action has now shifted from exclusivity of the inner sanctum where the fashion show was to be presented and spilled onto the streets, becoming interactive at the same time: 'You can hardly get up the steps at Lincoln Center, in New York, or walk along the Tuileries Garden path in Paris because of all the photographers snapping at the poseurs. Cameras point as wildly at their prey as those original paparazzi in Fellini's "La Dolce Vita".'

But here comes Suzy Menkes's harsh criticism regarding what she compares to a circus:

> Ah, fame! Or, more accurately in the fashion world, the celebrity circus of people who are famous for being famous. There are known mainly by their Facebook pages, their blogs and the fact that the street photographer Scott Schuman has immortalized them on his Sartorialist Web site. This photographer of 'real people' has spawned legions of imitators, just as the editors who dress for attention are now challenged by bloggers who dress for attention.

Harsh words indeed that focus on the fashion bloggers and fashion blogging which are not only about fame but financial gain (acquiring designer outfits from the designers as a form of advertising), free trips to fashion events, everything that Tavi Gevinson was offered for free, in exchange for which the bloggers have to blog (read: wax lyrically) about whatever or whoever finances or supports them, and Menkes points this out: 'Many bloggers are – or were – perceptive and succinct in their comments. But with the aim now to receive trophy gifts and paid-for trips to the next round of shows, only the rarest of bloggers could be seen as a critic in its original meaning of a visual and cultural arbiter.'

Thus, she concludes 'Fashion has to some extent become mob rule – or, at least, a survival of the most popular in a melee of crowdsourcing.' To go against these developments, Menkes concedes, would be 'doomed for failure', but she offers, no doubt with a wry smile, a solution: 'Perhaps the perfect answer would be to let the public preening go on out front, while the show moves, stealthily, to a different and secret venue, with the audience just a group of dedicated pros – dressed head to toe in black, of course.'

Going through the comments, what emerges is that mostly they are thoughtful, intelligent and full of praise for Suzy Menkes's courageous stance against celebrity culture but equally with an eye on attracting attention to themselves. In one of them Menkes herself (having published the article online) is called a blogger – by a blogger from France signing 'footagehead':

> Should one have some style to be an arbiter of style is the first thing that popped into my head as I read Ms. Menkes comments in her online post in TMagazine 'The Circus of Fashion' (Seeing as I read it online . . . is it not also a 'blog????'). Ms Menkes is herself then a blogger as defined by Wikipedia!
>
> Though I feel that Ms. Menkes did have some honest comments, I do feel they are a bit negative toward the new paradigm of 'blogging' brought on by technology. I feel fortunate to see the benefits of this new technology in my lifetime, in that everyone now has 'front row access' to whatever they want to see, and even in HD.

In many instances the bloggers have their own blogs or switched from journalism to blogging and have their own blogs. But of course, that rare blogger which Suzy Menkes mentions is the critic blogger, blogger critic? And here we have one such, Salomy from Amsterdam, charmingly naïve but genuine:

> I agree with Suzan (sic) Menkes [sic] quote: If fashion is for everyone, is it fashion? If you look at fashion as an art form, then it's not for everyone. Art you have to understand, so in fashion. Some people still understand fashion as an art form. Some other see it as a status object and there are people who don't have the visual feeling for fashion and they imitate the ones who truly understand fashion. So when somebody wears it is not straight fashion, but it is an expression. It is just like in the art world with painters. If somebody uses the action painting technique it's not directly an artist like Pollock. To become a journalist artist in fashion, you have to be one just like Suzan Menkes.

Yes, indeed Suzy Menkes: you are a 'journalist artist in fashion'.

CONCLUSION – WHERE TO FROM HERE?

The world wide web has revolutionized fashion, democratizing its sacred halls, making parades freely available for the first time in history, spreading the word instantaneously about any and every new trend, and delivering to our 'in box' any combination of blog, website or fashion film. Such sites still generally require words, even if simply a caption.

Although the availability of visual images of fashion has never been equalled, from museums digitizing much (although never all) of their collections, to bloggers 'lifting' images from old magazines or previously published books and avoiding copyright fees, the saturation of imagery in contemporary life does not seem to be matched by a comparable rise in the standard of writing or knowledge of history, and this fact is widely noted (Reponen, 2011; Granata, 2009). As Valerie Steele noted succinctly in her interview with the fashion critic Robin Givhan: 'Everyone's got opinions, but so what? If you want opinions, just ask a cab driver' (Steele, 2013, xiv).

We once read with great expectation the pronouncement of a world famous blogger who had arrived at Stockholm Fashion Week, only to discover that the insight for the day was regarding the high quality of the bathroom toiletries provided in the undoubtedly free hotel room in which (s)he was staying. Was that all there was to it? Or was it a Vreelandian or Warholian irony? Or *je ne sais quoi*?

As Caroline Evans points out in an essay that was published at the conclusion of our project: 'The intensification of image culture, and the capacity to connect at speed, have produced a new experience for the reader, so-called' (Evans, 2013, p. 78). Although optimistic regarding the image based 'cultural poetics' that are now possible via the web, Evans avoids any comment on the quality of contemporary fashion criticism generally. This is perhaps telling, as in a world obsessed with the image, there is more need than ever before for skilful interpretation and artful comment on these images – in words.

NOTES

Chapter 3

1 'John Trusler was a Church of England clergyman and author who came from a family of Wiltshire clothiers. He wrote a wide range of books on topics from gardening to politeness and the law, as well as *Hogarth Moralized* (1768) and a digested version of Lord Chesterfield's letters (1774) as *Principles of Politeness*. In 1775 he wrote the first English thesaurus.' Source: *Oxford Dictionary of National Biography*.

Chapter 7

1 A version of this essay was published by PMCN as '"Why Dont you"—Think for yourself? in Diana Vreeland after Diana Vreeland', special annual reviews issue of *Fasion Theory*, Volume 18, Issue 4, 2014, pp. 419–426.

2 We are grateful to Erika Lunding, freelance scholar, formerly of the Royal Library, Stockholm, for assistance with this entry. We also consulted Thomas Persson, Charlotte Rey and Anja Aronowsky Cronberg.

BIBLIOGRAPHY

Abrams, M. (2013), 'It's Tea Dress Time', *Financial Times*, 24 May, www.ft.com/intl/
    cms/s/2/29de9d18-bd8c–11e2-a735–00144feab7de.html#axzz2z9zO2Y4j
Acne Paper, 6th issue, summer 2008.
Addressing the Century (1998) Catalogue of the exhibition held at the Hayward Gallery,
    London, 8 October 1998 to 11 January 1999, with contributions by P. Wollen, J. Clark,
    U. Lehmann, C. Evans, R. Muir, J. Entwistle with E. Wilson, London: Hayward Gallery.
Alberti, L.B. (1970) *On Painting*, translated with introduction and notes by J.R. Spencer,
    New Haven and London: Yale University Press.
Appleby, J., Covington, E., Hoyt, D., Latham, M. and Sneider, A. (eds) (1996) *Knowledge
    and Postmodernism in Historical Perspective*, New York and London: Routledge.
Arnold, R. (2002) 'Looking American: Louise Dahl-Wolfe's Fashion Photographs of the
    1930s and 1940s', *Fashion Theory* 6 (1), March, pp. 45–60.
Ayer, A.J. (1971) *Language, Truth and Logic*, Harmondsworth: Penguin Books.
Barnard, M. (2002) *Fashion as Communication*, London and New York: Routledge.
Barnard, M. (ed.) (2007) *Fashion Theory: A Reader*, London: Routledge.
Barrett, C. (ed.) (1967) *Wittgenstein: Lectures and Conversations on Aesthetics,
    Psychology and Religious Belief*, Oxford: Blackwell.
Barthes, R. (1990) 'The Contest between Chanel and Courrèges, Refereed by a
    Philosopher' in R. Barthes, *The Language of Fashion*, translated by A. Stafford; edited
    by A. Stafford and M. Carter, Berkeley: University of California Press.
Baudelaire, C. (1972) *Selected Writings on Art and Artists*, Baltimore: Penguin Books.
Baudelaire, C. (1993) *The Flowers of Evil*, translated with notes by J. McGowan;
    introduction by J. Culler, Oxford: Oxford University Press.
Baudelaire, C. [1863] (1995) 'Le Peintre de la vie moderne XI: éloge du maquillage', in
    C. Baudelaire, *The Painter of Modern Life and Other Essays*, translated by J. Mayne,
    2nd ed., London and New York: Phaidon.
Baudelaire, C. (1998) *The Flowers of Evil*, Oxford: Oxford University Press.
Bazin, G. (1986) *Histoire de l'histoire de l'art (de Vasari à nos jours)*, Paris: Albin Michel.
Beardsley, M.C. (1966) *Aesthetics: From Classical Greece to the Present, a Short
    History*, New York: Macmillan.
Beiser, F.C. (ed.) (1995) *The Cambridge Companion to Hegel*, Cambridge: Cambridge
    University Press.
Bell, C. (2005) 'Significant Form' (extract from *Art*, 1914), in N. Warburton (ed.),
    Philosophy, London and New York, Routledge, pp. 475–9.
Benson, H. (ed.) (2009) *A Companion to Plato*, Chichester: Wiley-Blackwell.
Blunt, A. (1973) *Artistic Theory in Italy 1450–1600*, Oxford: Oxford University Press.
Blunt, A. (1991) *Art and Architecture in France 1500–1700*, London: Pelican History of
    Art, Penguin.

Bolton, A. and Harold, K. (eds) (2012) *Schiaparelli and Prada (Impossible Conversations)*, introduced by J. Thurman, published in conjunction with exhibition of same title at The Metropolitan Museum of Art, New York, 10 May to 19 August 2012, New York: Metropolitan Museum of Art.

Bourdieu, P. and Delsaut, Y. (1975) 'Le Couturier et sa griffe: contribution à une théorie de la magique', *Actes de la recherche en sciences sociales* 1 (1), pp. 7–36.

Breward, C. (1994) 'Femininity and Consumption: the Problem of the Late Nineteenth-Century Fashion Journal', *Journal of Design History* 7 (2), pp. 71–89.

Brusatin, M. (1986) *Histoire des couleurs*, Paris: Flammarion.

Burke, E. (1990) *A Philosophical Enquiry into the Origin of our Ideas of the Sublime and the Beautiful*, Oxford: Oxford University Press.

Butcher, S.H. (1951) *Aristotle's Theory of Poetry and Fine Art*, 4th edn, New York: Dover.

Clark, J. and Frisa, M.L. (2012) *Diana Vreeland after Diana Vreeland*, Palazzo Fortuny, Venice, 10 March to 25 June, Venice: Marsilio Editori.

Collins, P. (1971) *Architectural Judgement*, London: Faber & Faber.

Collins English Dictionary (2005) Glasgow: HarperCollins.

Conekin, B. and de la Haye, A. (eds) (2006) 'Fashion Theory', *Vogue*, special double issue, March–June.

Cooper, D. (ed.) (1995) *A Companion to Aesthetics*, Oxford: Blackwell.

Cooper, J.M. (ed.) (1997) *Plato: Complete Works*, Indianapolis: Cambridge Hackett Publishing.

Cropper, E. (1998) 'Introduction', in F. Ames-Lewis and M. Rogers (eds), *Concepts of Beauty in Renaissance Art*, Aldershot: Ashgate, pp. 1–11.

Delon, M. (ed.) (2008) *Diderot: Salons*, Paris: Gallimard.

Descartes, R. (1969) *Philosophical Writings*, translated and edited by E. Anscombe and P. Thomas Geach, London: Nelson.

Doney, W. (ed.) (1968) *Descartes: A Collection of Critical Essays*, London: Macmillan.

Esten, J. (2001) *Diana Vreeland: Bazaar Years, Including 100 Audacious Why Don't Yous. . .?*, New York: Universe and Rizzoli.

Evans, C. (2013) 'Yesterday's Emblems and Tomorrow's Commodities: the Return of the Repressed in Fashion Imagery Today', in S. Bruzzi and P.C. Gibson (eds), *Fashion Cultures Revisited*, London and New York: Routledge.

Evans, C. and Thornton, M. (1989) *Women and Fashion: A New Look*, London: Quartet.

Farge, A. (1994) *Subversive Words. Public Opinion in Eighteenth-Century France*, Cambridge: Polity Press.

Feagin, S. and Maynard, P. (eds) (1997) *Aesthetics*, Oxford: Oxford University Press.

Frankel, S. 'Yohji', *Independent*, 14 April 2005.

Fukai, A. et al. (2002) *Fashion: A History from the 18th to the 20th Century*, the Collection of the Kyoto Costume Institute, Cologne: Taschen.

Furbank, P.N. and Cain, A. (2004) *Mallarmé on Fashion: A Translation of the Fashion Magazine La Dernière Mode, With Commentary*, Oxford and New York: Berg.

Gaut, B.N. and Lopes, D.M. (eds) (2001) *The Routledge Companion to Aesthetics*, London: Routledge.

Gill, A. (1998) 'Deconstruction Fashion: the Making of Unfinished, Decomposing and Re-assembled Clothes', *Fashion Theory* 2 (1), March.

Granata, F. (ed.) (2009) *Fashion Projects, No. 4: On Fashion Criticism*, New York: New York Foundation of the Arts.

Grayling A.C. (ed.) (1995) *Philosophy (A Guide Through the Subject)*, Oxford: Oxford University Press.

Greig, H. (2013) *The Beau Monde: Fashionable Society in Georgian London*, Oxford: Oxford University Press.

Groom, G. (2013) *L'Impressionnisme et la Mode*, Paris: Skira Flammarion.

Hanfling, O. (ed.) (1992) *Philosophical Aesthetics (An Introduction)*, Oxford: Blackwell.

Harrison, C., Wood, P. and Gaiger, J (eds) (2000) *Art in Theory 1648–1815: An Anthology of Changing Ideas*, Oxford: Blackwell.

Hiltunen, A. (2002) *Aristotle In Hollywood: The Anatomy of a Successful Storytelling*, Bristol: Intellect Books.

Hobbes, T. (1985) *Leviathan*, London: Penguin Books.

Hollander, A. (1993) *Seeing Through Clothes*, Los Angeles and London: University of California Press.

Holt, E.G. (ed.) (1957, 1958, 1966) *A Documentary History of Art*, 3 vols, New York: Doubleday Anchor.

Honour, H. and Fleming, J. (1982) *A World History of Art*, London: Macmillan.

Hume, D. (1965) *Of the Standard of Taste and Other Essays*, New York: The Bobbs-Merrill Company.

Hume, D. (1977) *An Enquiry Concerning Human Understanding*, Classics of Western Philosophy, Indianapolis: Hackett Publishing Company.

Huysmans, K. (1971) *Against Nature*, Harmondsworth: Penguin Books.

Israel, J. (2008) *Enlightenment Contested: Philosophy, Modernity, and the Emancipation of Man 1670–1752*, Oxford: Oxford University Press.

Jones, J.M. (2004) *Sexing la Mode: Gender, Fashion and Commercial Culture in Old Regime France*, Oxford: Berg.

Jung, C.G. (1971) *Memories, Dreams, Reflections*, Fontana Library Theology and Philosophy, London: Collins.

Kant, I. (1966) *Critique of Judgement*, translated by J.H. Bernard, New York and London: Hafner Publishing.

Koda, H. and Bolton, A. (eds) (2007) *Poiret*, catalogue for *Poiret: King of Fashion*, exhibition held at Metropolitan Museum of Art, New York, New Haven and London: Yale University Press.

Kristeller, P.O. (1961) *Renaissance Thought II*, Papers on Humanism and the Arts, New York: Harper Torchbooks.

Langlade, J. de (1997) *Oscar Wilde: Stéphane Mallarmé: Noblesse de la Robe*, Paris: Les Belles Lettres.

Lehmann, U. (2000) *Tigersprung: Fashion in Modernity*, Cambridge, MA: MIT Press.

Lessing, G.E. (1967) *Laocoön, Nathan the Wise* and *Minna von Barnhelm*, translated by W.A. Steel and A.A. Dent, Everyman's Library, London: Dent.

Longinus (1963) *On the Sublime*, translated by H.L. Havell, Everyman's Library, London: Dutton; New York: Dent.

Lynge-Jorlen, A. (2012) 'Between Frivolity and Art: Contemporary Niche Fashion Magazines', *Fashion Theory* 16 (1), March, pp. 7–28.

M'Laren, L. (1887) 'On the Fallacy of the Superiority of Men', *The Woman's World*, December.

McDowell, C. (1986) 'The Vreeland Version', *Country Life*, 15 May, pp. 1394–5.

McKeon, R. (ed.) (2001) *The Basic Works of Aristotle*, New York: The Modern Library.

Mackie, E. (1997) *Market à la Mode: Fashion, Commodity and Gender in the Tatler and the Spectator*, Baltimore and London: Johns Hopkins University Press.

McNeil, P. (2011) 'Haute Couture Within a Fashion Studies Perspective', Swedish translated from English, in F. Andersson (ed.), *Kunglig Vintage [Royal Vintage]*, Stockholm: Livrustkammaren, pp. 182–93.

McQueen, A. (2011) *Empress Eugénie and the Arts*, Farnham: Ashgate.

Martin, R. (1997) 'A Note, A Charismatic Art: The Balance of Ingratiation and Outrage in Contemporary Fashion', *Fashion Theory* 1 (1), pp. 91–104.

Martin, R. (1998a) 'A Note: Gianni Versace's Anti-Bourgeois Little Black Dress', *Fashion Theory* 2 (1), March, pp. 95–100.

Martin, R. (1998b) *Cubism and Fashion*, exhibition catalogue, New York: Metropolitan Museum of Art.

Mayhew, A. (ed.) (n.d.) newspaper clipping, no date, no place, reproduced in 'Resort Life, Chapter XXXV: June–December, Down East + Palm Beach', in 'The Archive of Ellen Glendinning Fraser Ordway' [1968]; *New York Social Diary*, viewed 2014 www.newyorksocialdiary.com/node/1910514.

Mayne, J. (ed.) (1965) *Art in Paris, 1845–1862: Salons and other Exhibitions Reviewed by Charles Baudelaire*, Ithaca, NY: Cornell University Press.

Mendes, V. and de la Haye, A. (1999) *20th Century Fashion*, London: Thames and Hudson.

Meyer, U. (1972) *Conceptual Art*, New York: E.P. Dutton.

Miller, S. (2007) 'Fashion as Art; Is Fashion Art?' *Fashion Theory* 11 (1), pp. 25–40.

Miller, S. (2013) 'Taste, Fashion and the French Fashion Magazine', in D. Bartlett, S. Cole and A. Rocamora (eds), *Fashion Media Past and Present*, London: Bloomsbury, pp. 13–21.

Monk, R. and Raphael, F. (eds) (2001) *The Great Philosophers*, London: Phoenix.

Morini, E. (2006) *Storia della moda: XVIII–XX secolo*, Milan: Skira.

Muir, R. (2002) 'When I Die, I Want to Go to Vogue', in R. Derrick and R. Muir (eds), *Unseen Vogue: The Secret History of Fashion Photography*, London: Little, Brown and Condé Nast.

Murdoch, R. (1977) *The Fire and the Sun: Why Plato Banished the Artists*, Oxford: Oxford University Press

Nussbaum, M.C. (1989) *The Fragility of Goodness: Luck and Ethics in Greek Tragedy and Philosophy*, Cambridge: Cambridge University Press

L'Officiel de la couture, de la mode de Paris, organ de propaganda et d'expression de l'art Français (1940) March.

Pater, W. (1961) *The Renaissance*, London: Fontana/Collins.

Payne, M. (ed.) (1997) *A Dictionary of Cultural and Critical Theory*, Oxford: Blackwell.

Reponen, J. (2011) 'Fashion Criticism Today?', in A. de Witt-Paul and M. Crouch (eds), *Fashion Forward*, Oxford: Interdisciplinary Press ebook.

Reynolds, J. (1969) *Discourses on Art*, London: Collier Books.

Rocamora, A. (2011) 'Personal Fashion Blogs: Screens and Mirrors in Digital Self-portraits', *Fashion Theory* 15 (4), pp. 407–24.

Rocamora, A. (2013) 'How New Are New Media? The Case of Fashion Blogs', in D. Bartlett, Shaun C. and A. Rocamora (eds) *Fashion Media Past and Present*, London: Bloomsbury, pp.155–64.

Ross, J.B. and McLaughlin, M.M. (eds) (1977) *The Portable Renaissance Reader,* Harmondsworth: Penguin Books.

Rossi-Camus, J. (2012) 'DV: an Edited Chronology', in J. Clark and M.L. Frisa (eds), *Diana Vreeland after Diana Vreeland*, exhibition at Palazzo Fortuny, Venice, 10 March to 25 June, Venice: Marsilio Editori, pp. 211–13.

Rowlands, P. (2005) *A Dash of Daring: Carmel Snow and Her Life in Fashion, Art, and Letters*, New York, London, Toronto, Sydney: Atria Books.

Russell, B. (1979) *History of Western Philosophy: and its Connection with Political and Social Circumstances from the Earliest Times to the Present Day*, London: Unwin Paperbacks.

Seeling, C. (2000) *Fashion: The Century of the Designer, 1900–1999*, Cologne: Könemann.

Shakespeare, W. (1980) *The Complete Works of William Shakespeare*, the Cambridge Text established by J. Dover Wilson for Cambridge University Press, London: Octopus.

Shaw, S. (n.d.) 'How to Be Ironic', http://uk.askmen.com/money/how_to_400/469_be-ironic.html.

Simon, M. (1995) *Mode et peinture: le Second Empire et l'impressionisme*, Paris: Editions Hazan; English edition published in 1995 as *Fashion in Art: the Second Empire and Impressionism*, translated by E. Jephcott, London: Zwemmer.

Sotheby's (1990) *Property from the Estate of Diana D. Vreeland*, New York, 19 April.

Spencer, R. (1970) *Leon Battiosta Alberti: On Painting*, New Haven and London: Yale University Press.

Steele, V. (2013) 'In Conversation with Robin Givhan, Fashion and Culture Critic, The Washington Post, Newsweek, The Guardian', *Vestoj: The Journal of Sartorial Matters* 4, 'On Power', pp. xi–xvii.

Steele, V. and Park, J. (2008) *Gothic: Dark Glamour*, New York: Yale University Press and Fashion Institute of Technology.

Stuart, A.M. (2012) *Empress of Fashion. A Life of Diana Vreeland*, New York: Harper Collins.

Teukolsky, R. (2009) *The Literate Eye: Victorian Art Writing and Modernist Aesthetics*, New York: Oxford University Press.

Thompson, J.B. (1990) *Ideology and Modern Culture: Critical Social Theory in the Era of Mass Communication*, Stanford: Stanford University Press.

Trusler, J. [1735–1820] 'Memoirs, part II', undated, c.1791, unpublished MS, vol. 71, Lewis Walpole Library, Yale University, no pagination.

Van Dijk, S. (1981) 'Femmes et journaux au XVIIIe siècle', in *La Presse aux XVII et XVIII siècles*, special issue of *Australian Journal of French Studies*, pp. 164–78.

Vasari, G. (1997) *Le vite dei più eccellenti pittori, scultori é architetti*, Rome: Grandi Tascabili Economici Newton.

Vasari, G. (1963) *Lives of the Painters, Sculptors and Architects*, 4 vols, translated by A.B. Hinds, Everyman's Library: New York: Dutton.

Virgil (2002) *The Aeneid: Book II*, translated by A.S. Kline, www.poetryintranslation.com/PITBR/Latin/VirgilAeneidII.htm.

Vreeland, D. (1984) *DV*, edited by G. Plimpton and C. Hemphill, London: Weidenfeld and Nicolson.

Vreeland, A. (ed.) (2013) *Diana Vreeland, Memos: The* Vogue *Years, 1962–1971*, New York: Rizzoli.

Watkin, D (1986) *A History of Western Architecture*, London: Laurence King.

Wickham, G. (1994) *A History of the Theatre*, London: Phaidon Press.

Wilde, O. (1968) *Complete Works of Oscar Wilde*, introduction by V. Holland, London and Glasgow: Collins.

Wilenski, R.H. (1973) *French Painting*, New York: Dover.

Wittgenstein, L. (1967) *Lectures and Conversations on Aesthetics, Psychology and Religious Belief*, Oxford: Basil Blackwell.

Wollen, P. (1998) *Addressing the Century: 100 Years of Art and Fashion*, London: Hayward Gallery.

INDEX